AF496638

LANDCASTER PRESS

Beauty

Volume Fifteen

Thomas G. Jewusiak

Jacket Design by Thomas G. Jewusiak

Cover Art by Thomas G. Jewusiak

All art, including clothing, contained herein, by Thomas G. Jewusiak

First Hard Cover Edition

First Printing

Jewusiak, Thomas G.

Beauty

Volume Fifteen

ISBN: 979-8-9912851-5-5

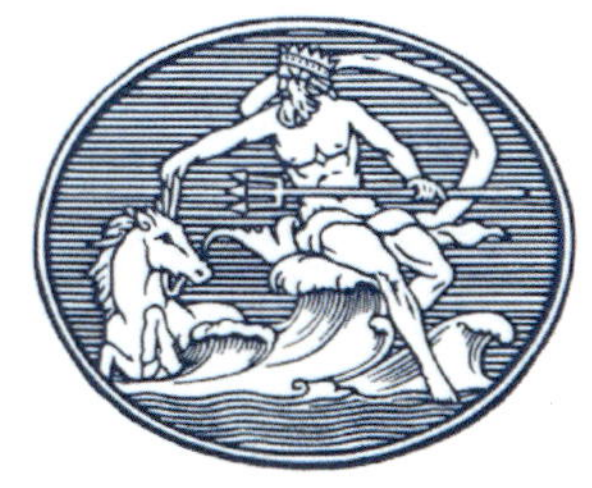

LANDCASTER PRESS

West Palm Beach

LandcasterPress.com

LandcasterPress@aol.com

Beauty is one of the most universal and timeless themes in art. Throughout history, artists have been fascinated by the human form, especially the female form, and have tried to capture its essence and express its meaning in various ways. Beauty is not only a matter of aesthetics, but also a matter of culture, values, emotions, and ideals. Beauty is subjective, relative, and dynamic. What is considered beautiful in one era, place, or society may not be in another. Beauty is also influenced by the personal preferences, experiences, and tastes of the artists and the viewers.

In this book, I present a selection of my paintings that explore the concept of beauty in different historical periods and artistic movements. I have been a working professional painter all of my adult life, and I have always been interested in the history of art and the evolution of female beauty in art. I have studied the works of the masters and learned from their techniques, styles, and visions. I have also developed my own style of painting that combines realism, impressionism, and fantasy. I use realistic details, impressionistic colors, and fantastical elements to create my own interpretations of beauty.

My paintings are not meant to be exact copies or reproductions of the original artworks, but rather my personal homage and tribute to them. I do not intend to imitate or compete with the masters, but to express my admiration and appreciation for their art. I also do not intend to make any definitive statements or judgments about beauty, but to invite the viewers to explore and enjoy the diversity and richness of beauty in art.

I hope that this book will inspire you to discover and appreciate the beauty of art and the beauty of women in all their forms and expressions. I hope that this book will also inspire you to create your own beauty and share it with the world.

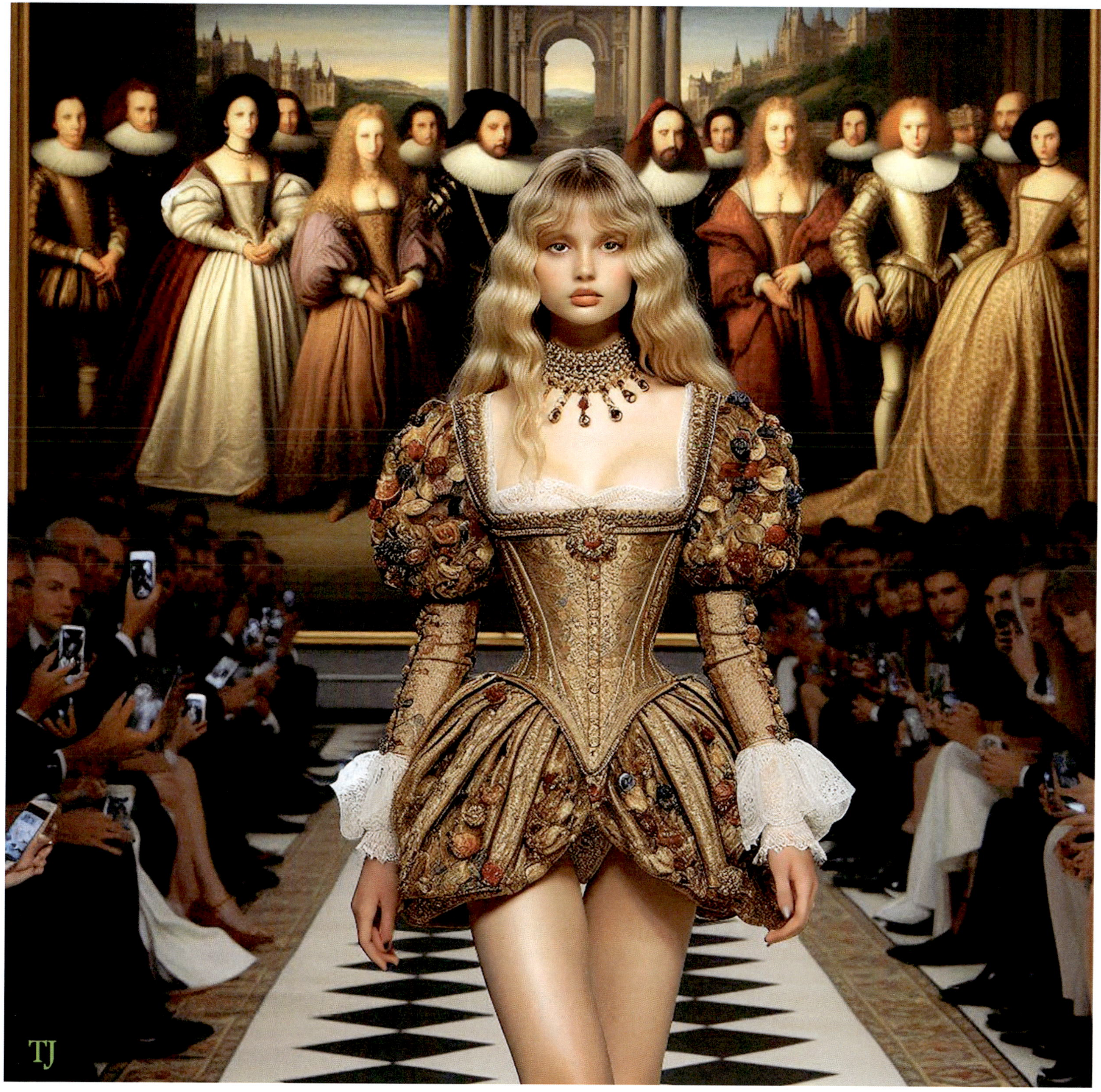
TJ

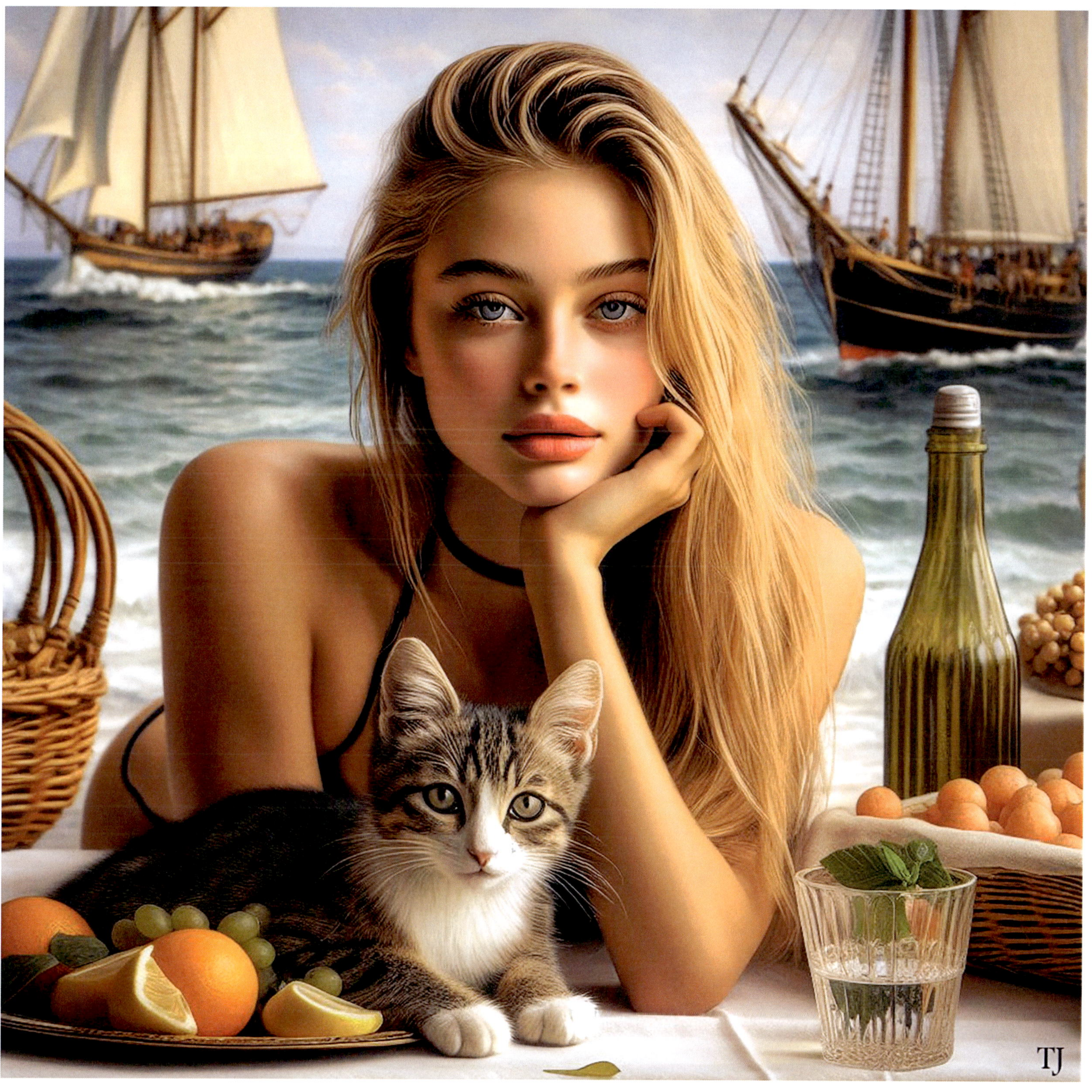

TJ

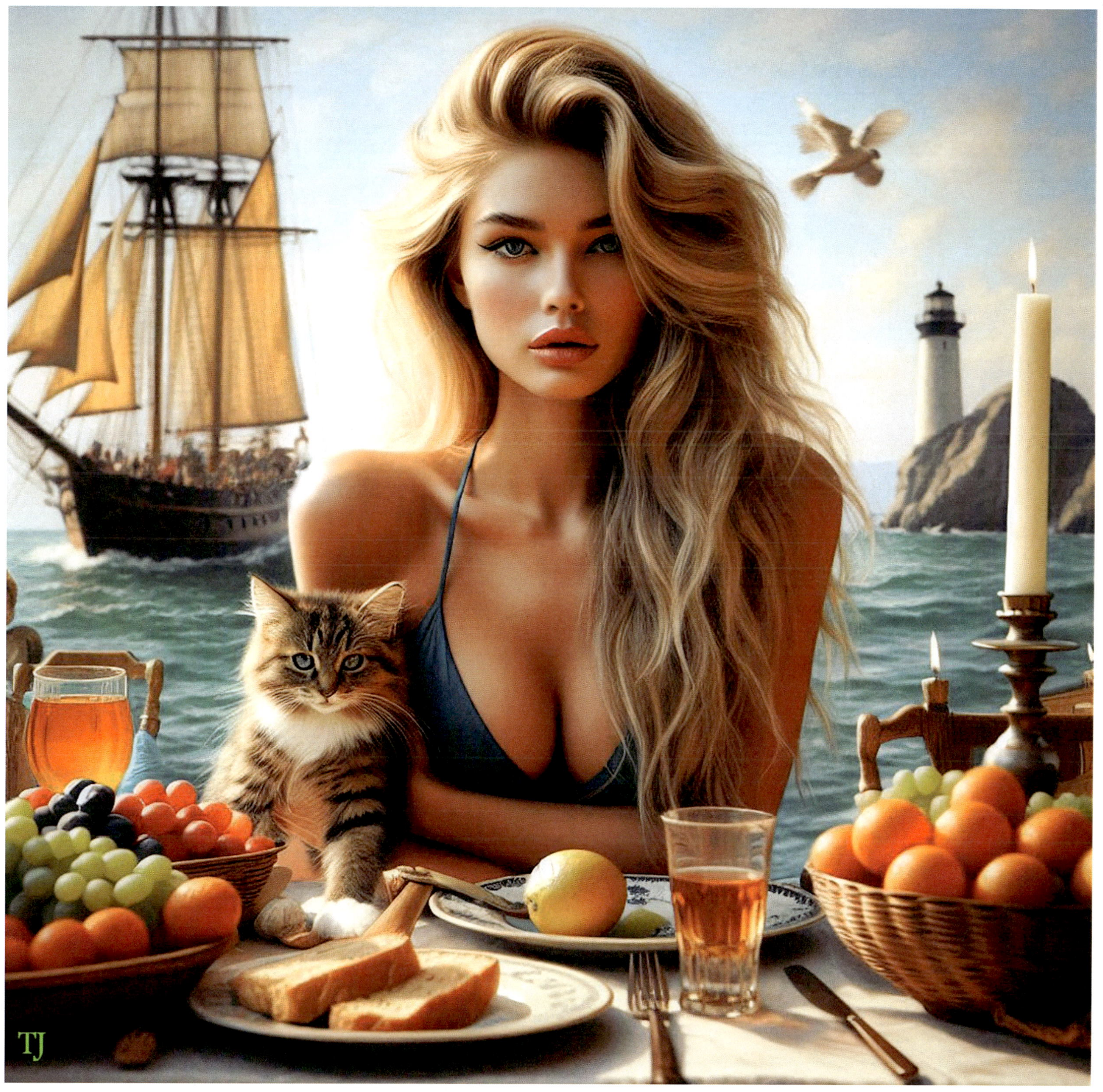

TJ

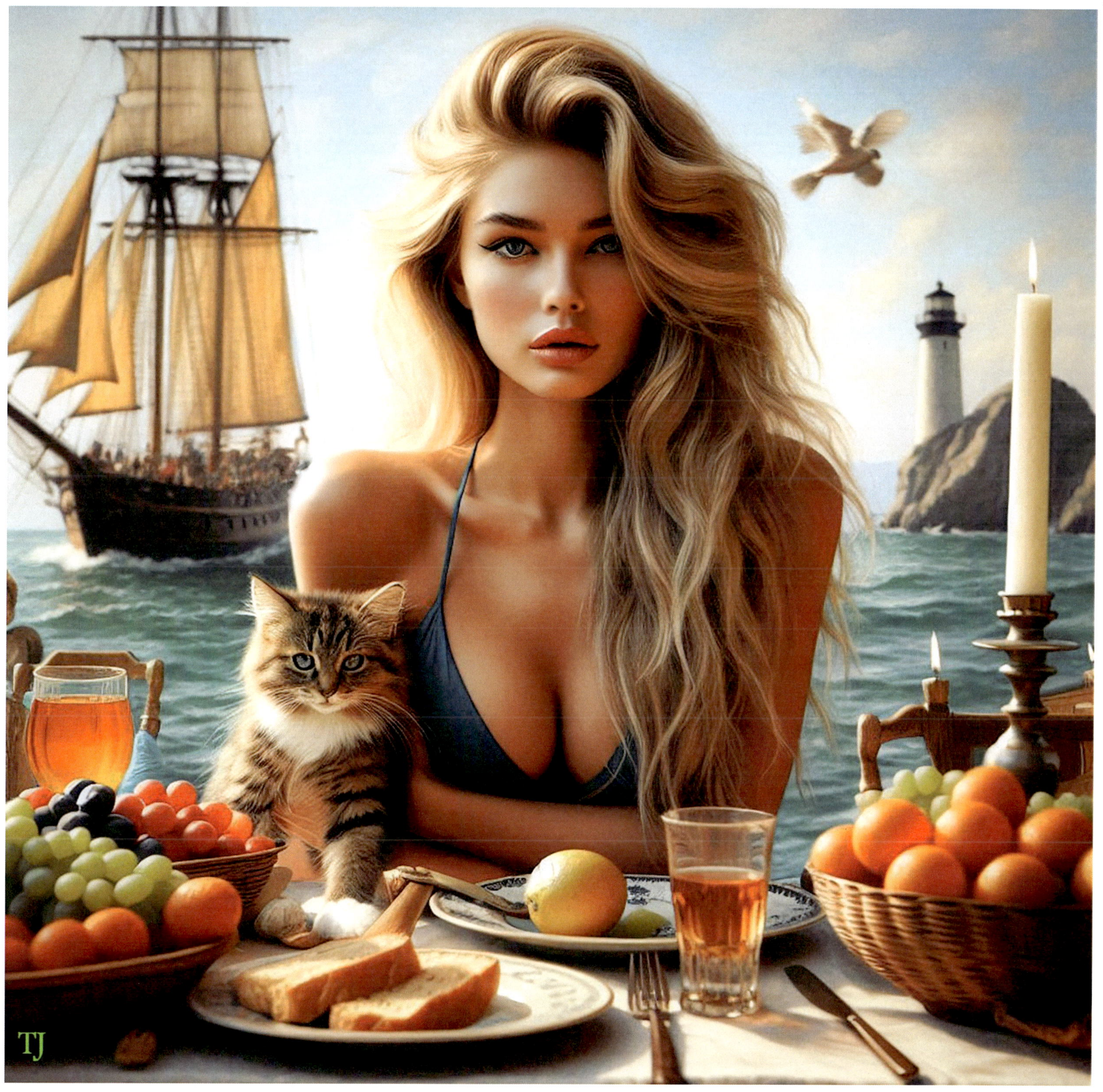
TJ

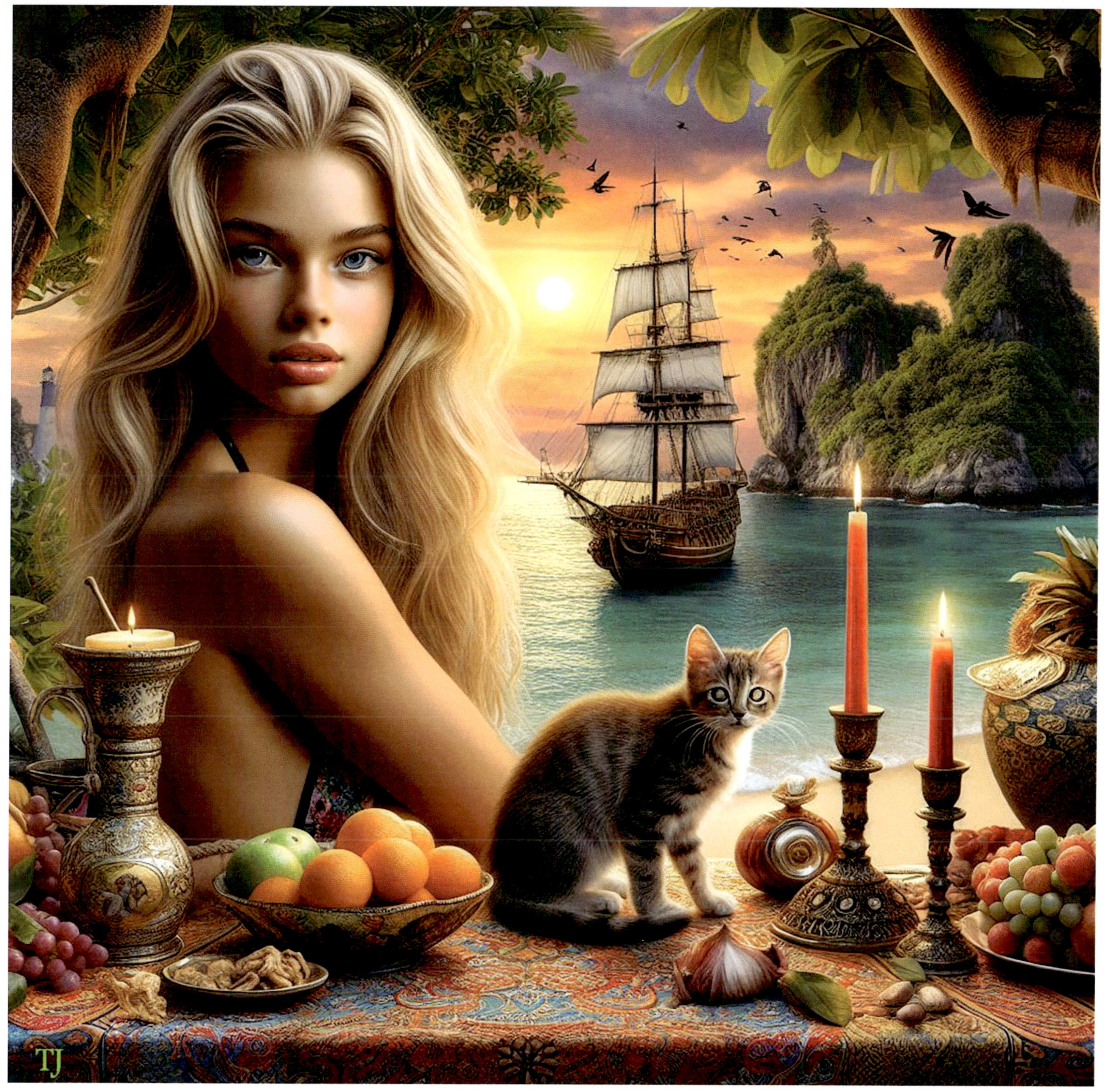

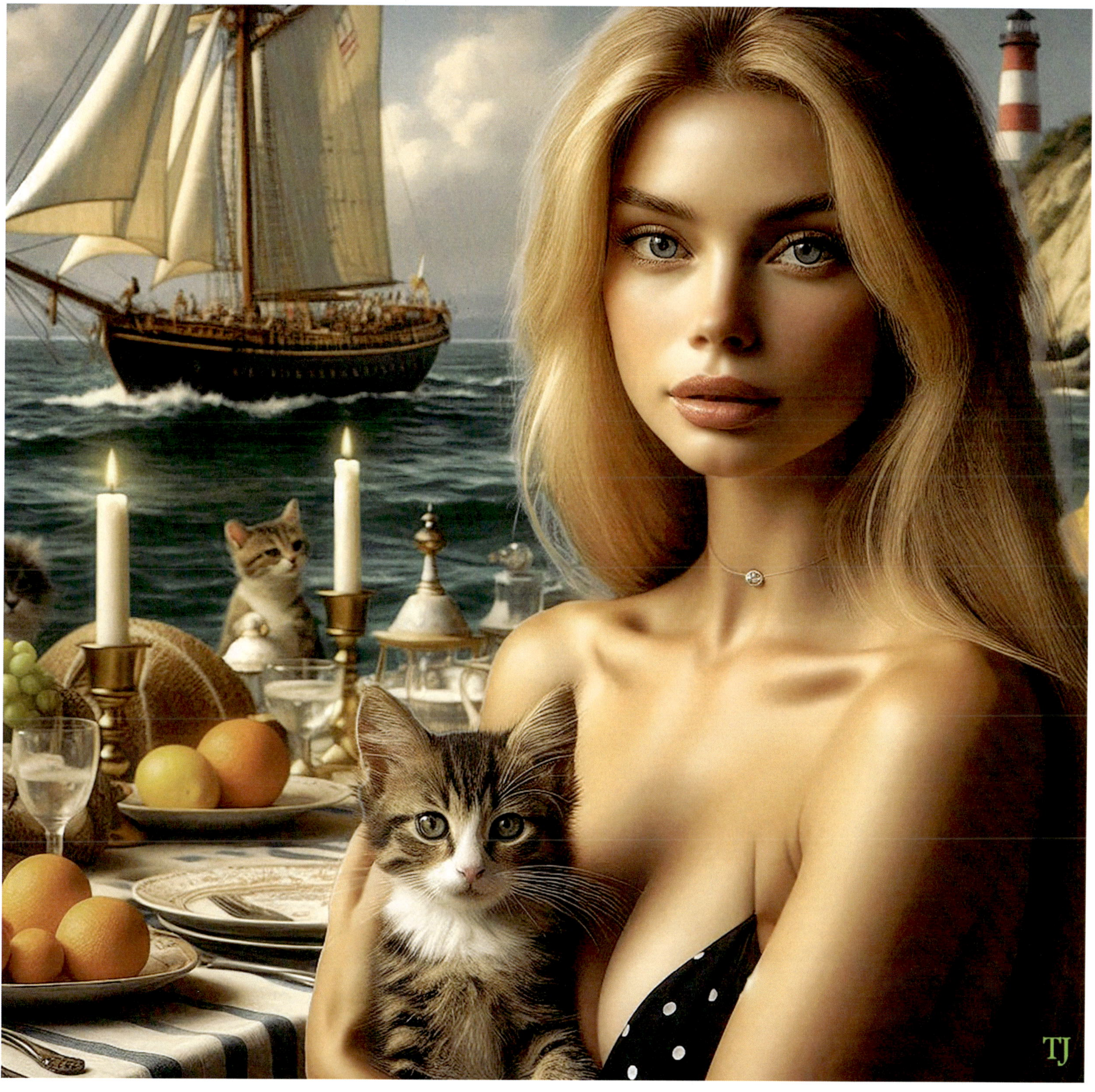

TJ

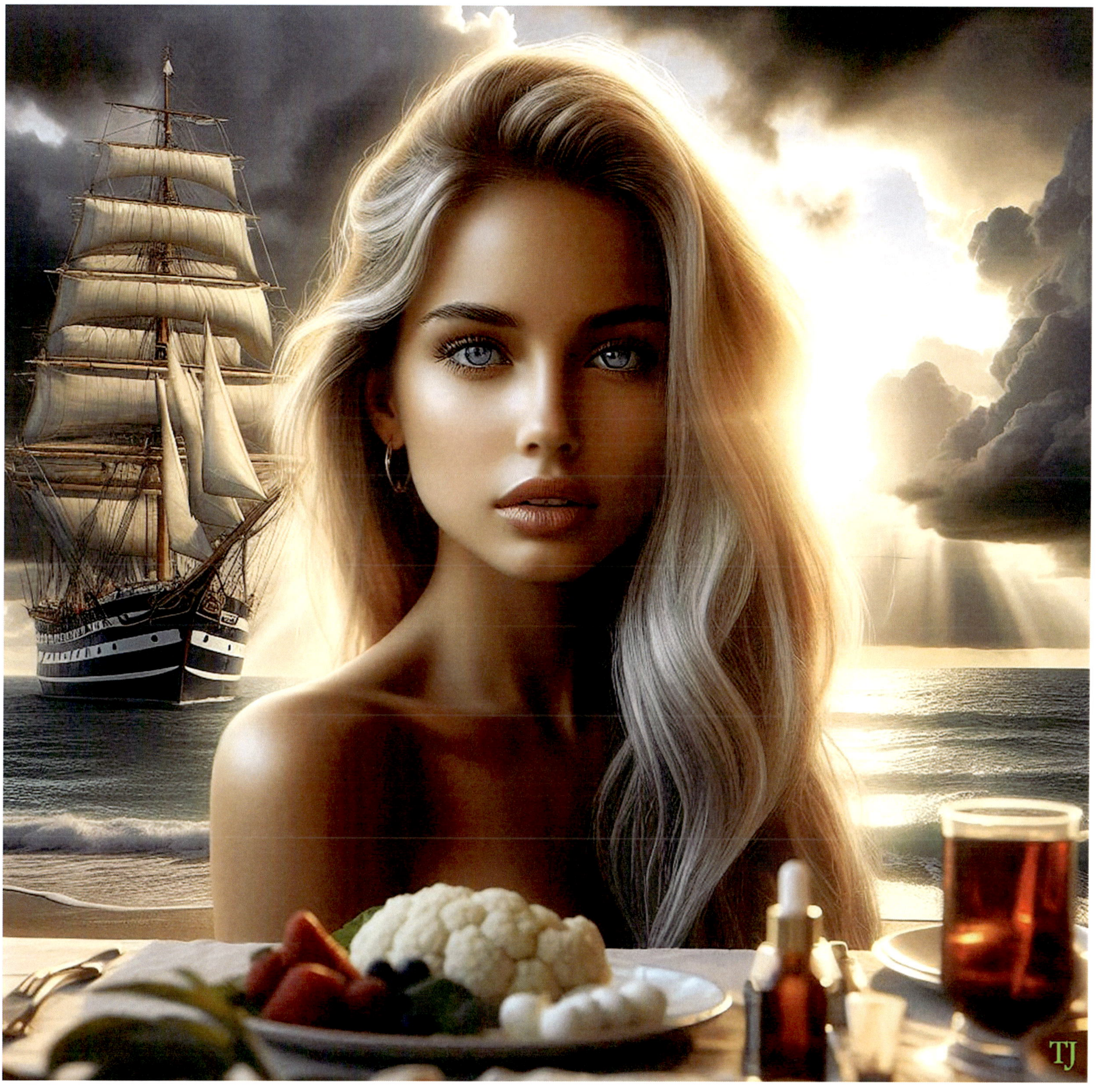

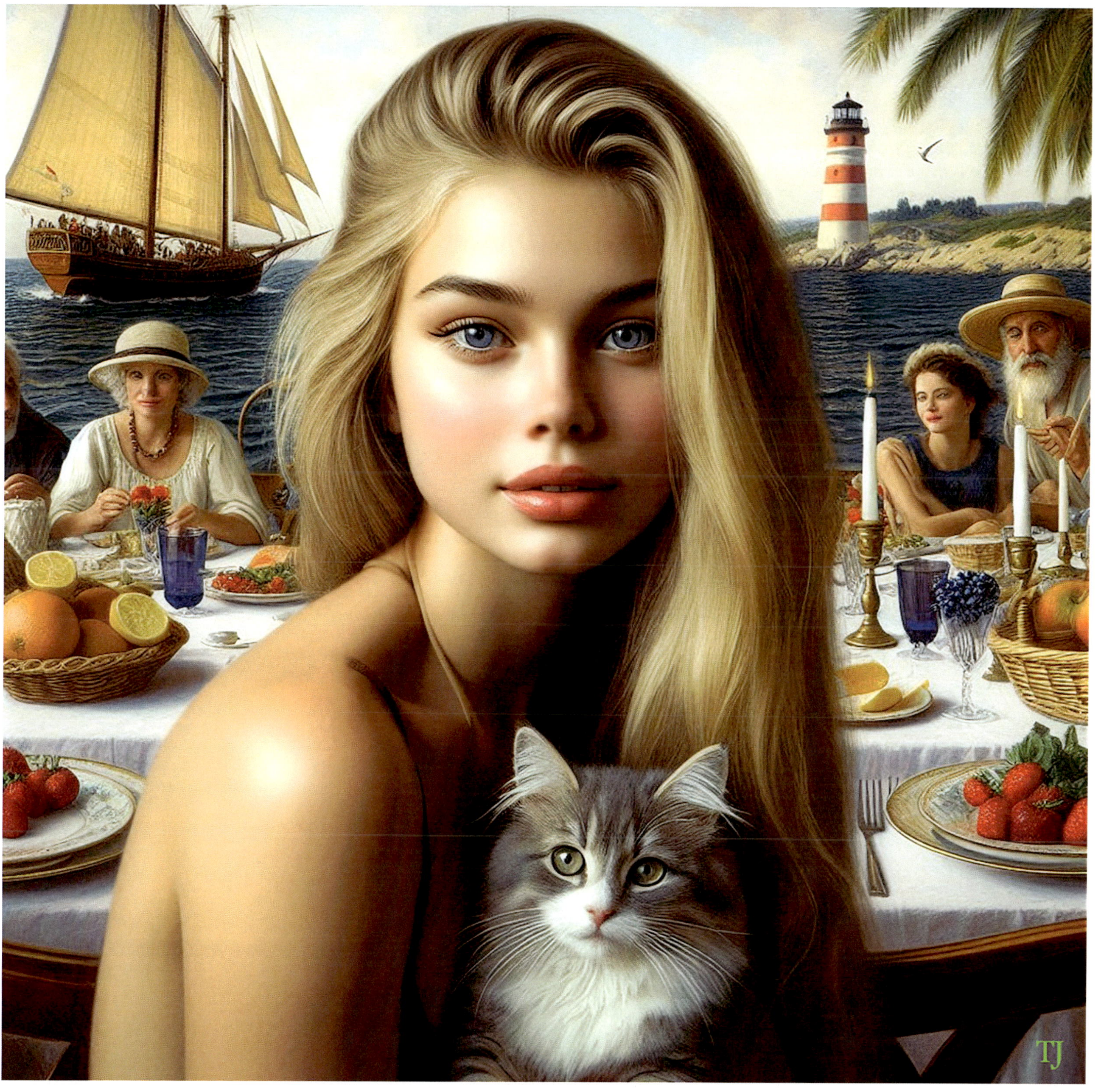

TJ

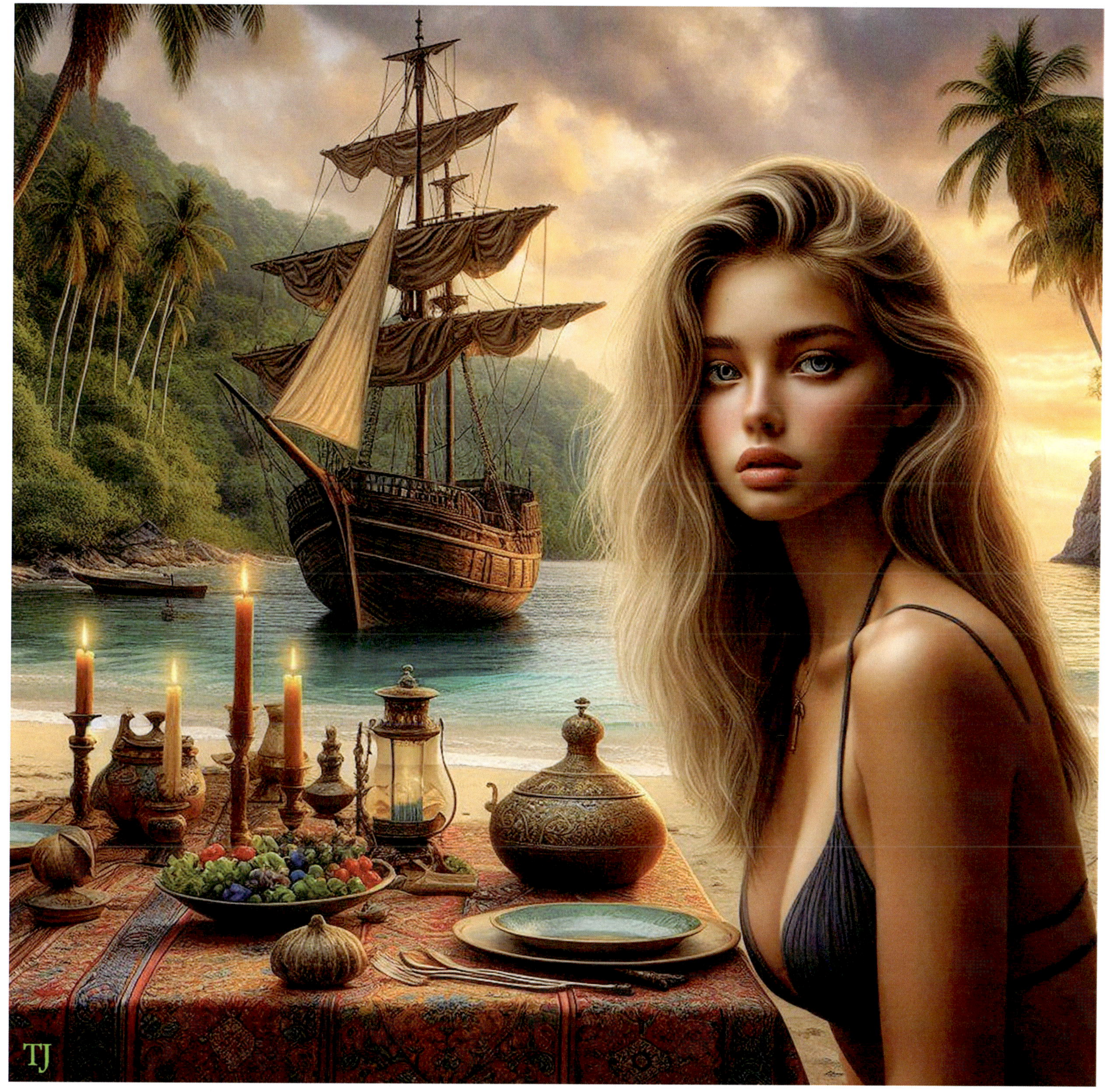
TJ

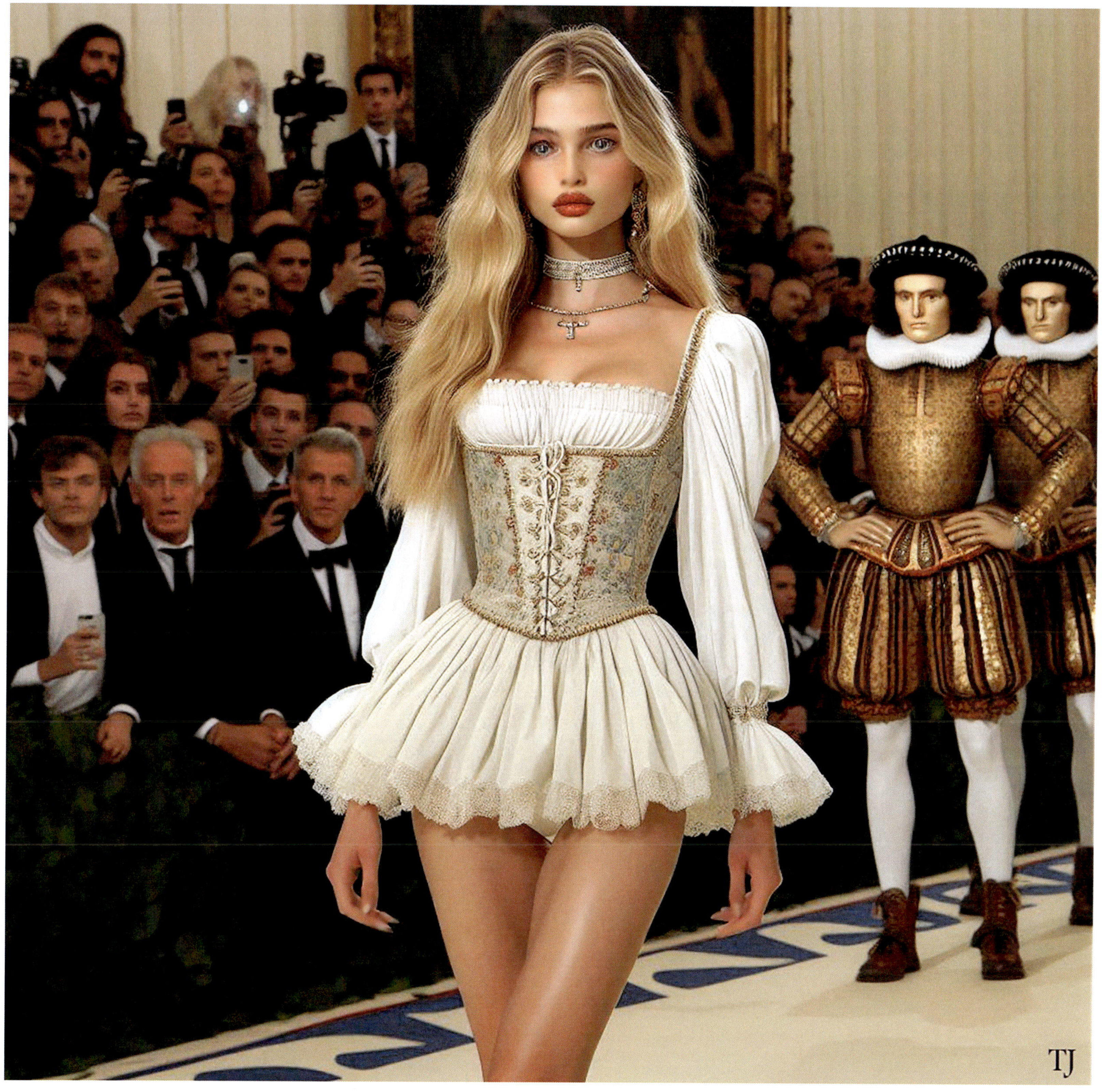
TJ

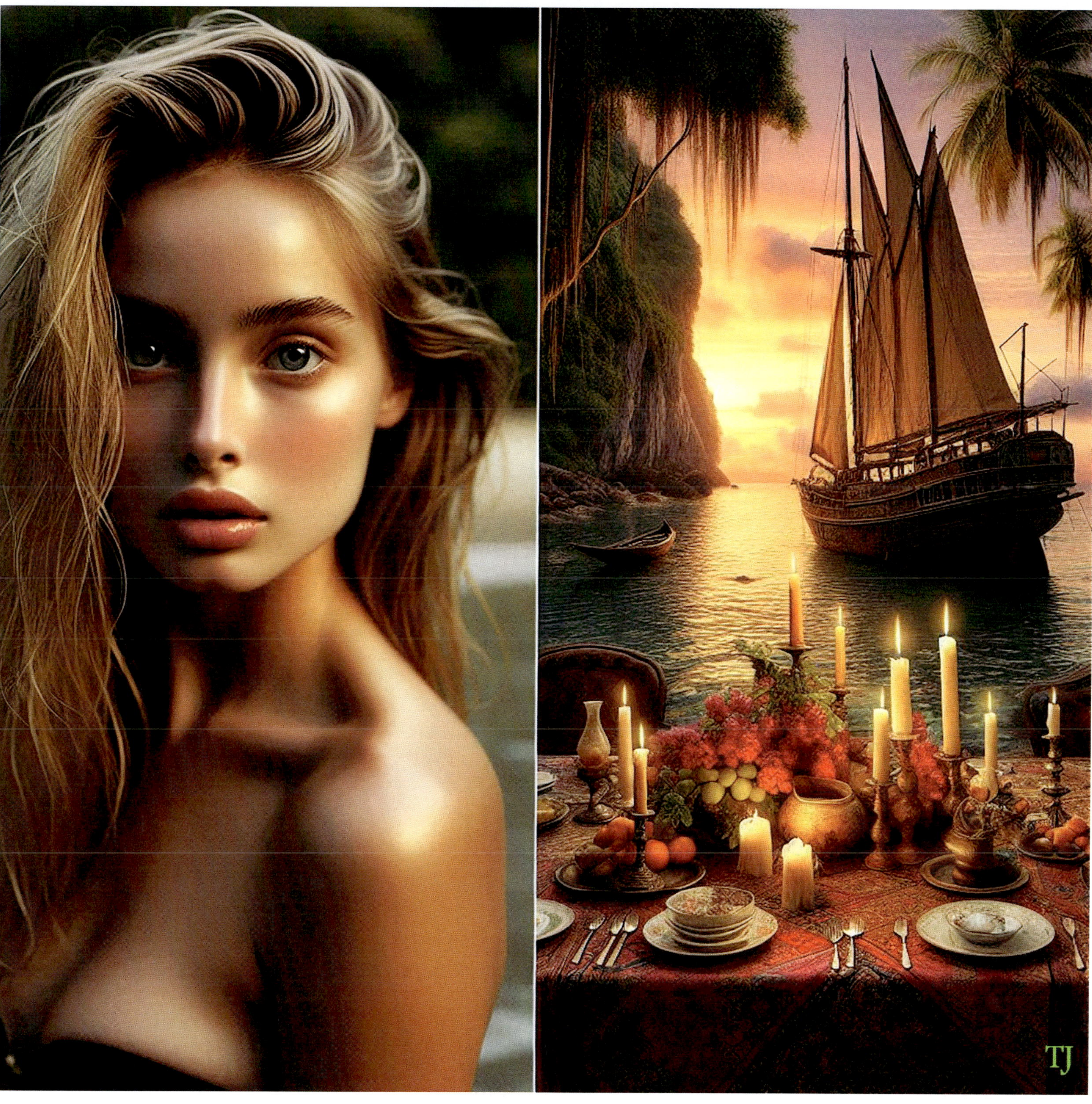

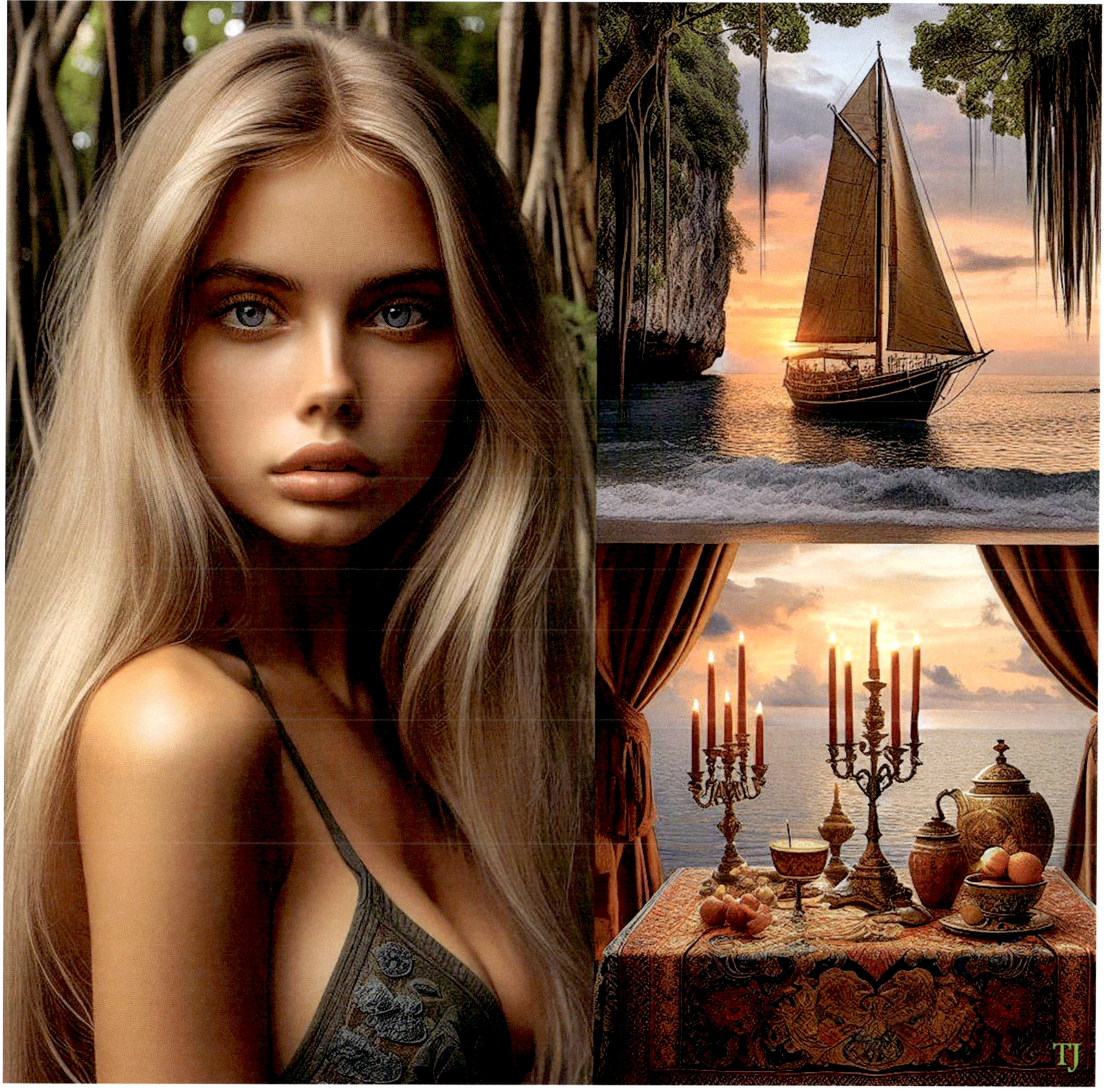

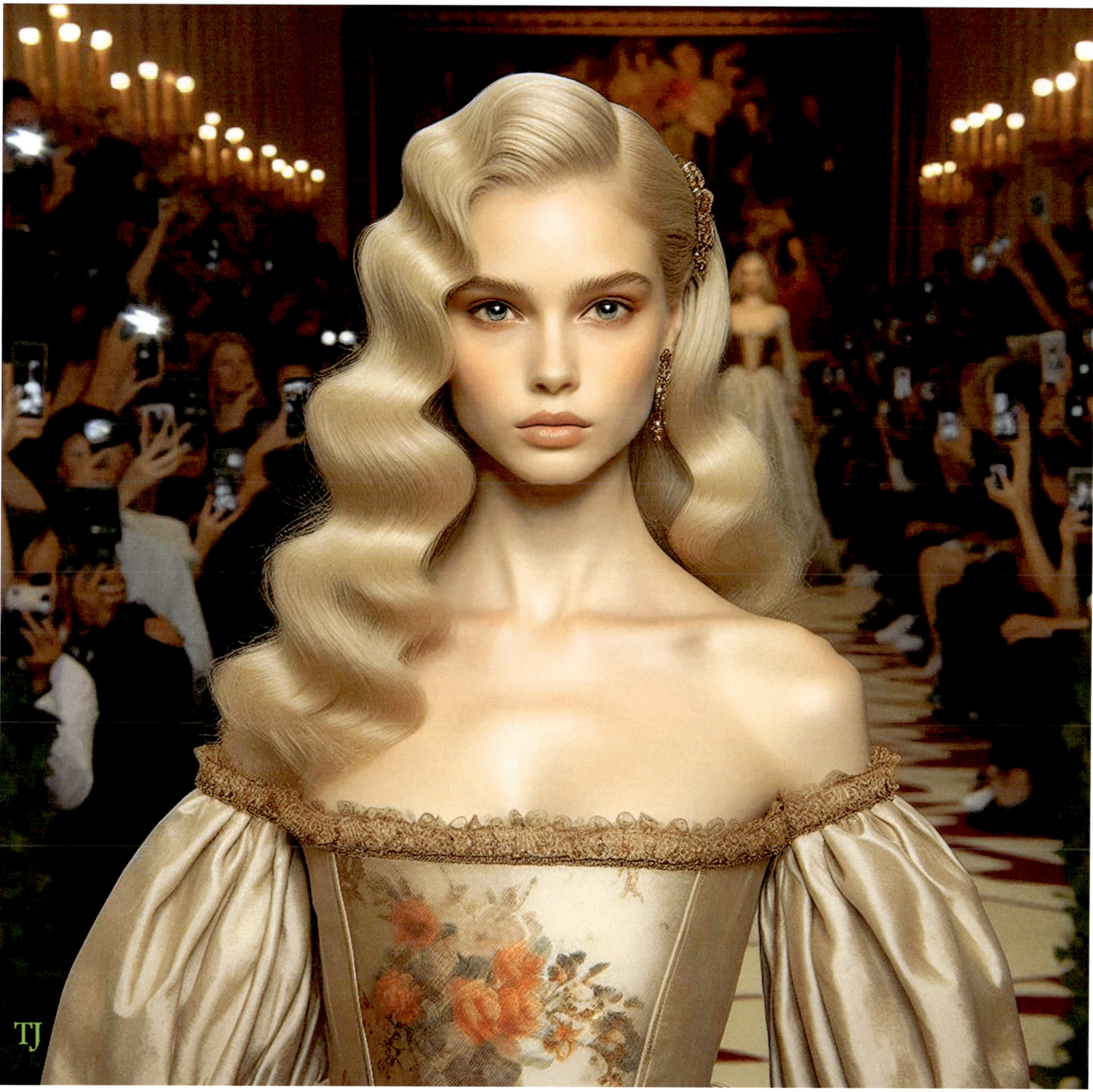
TJ

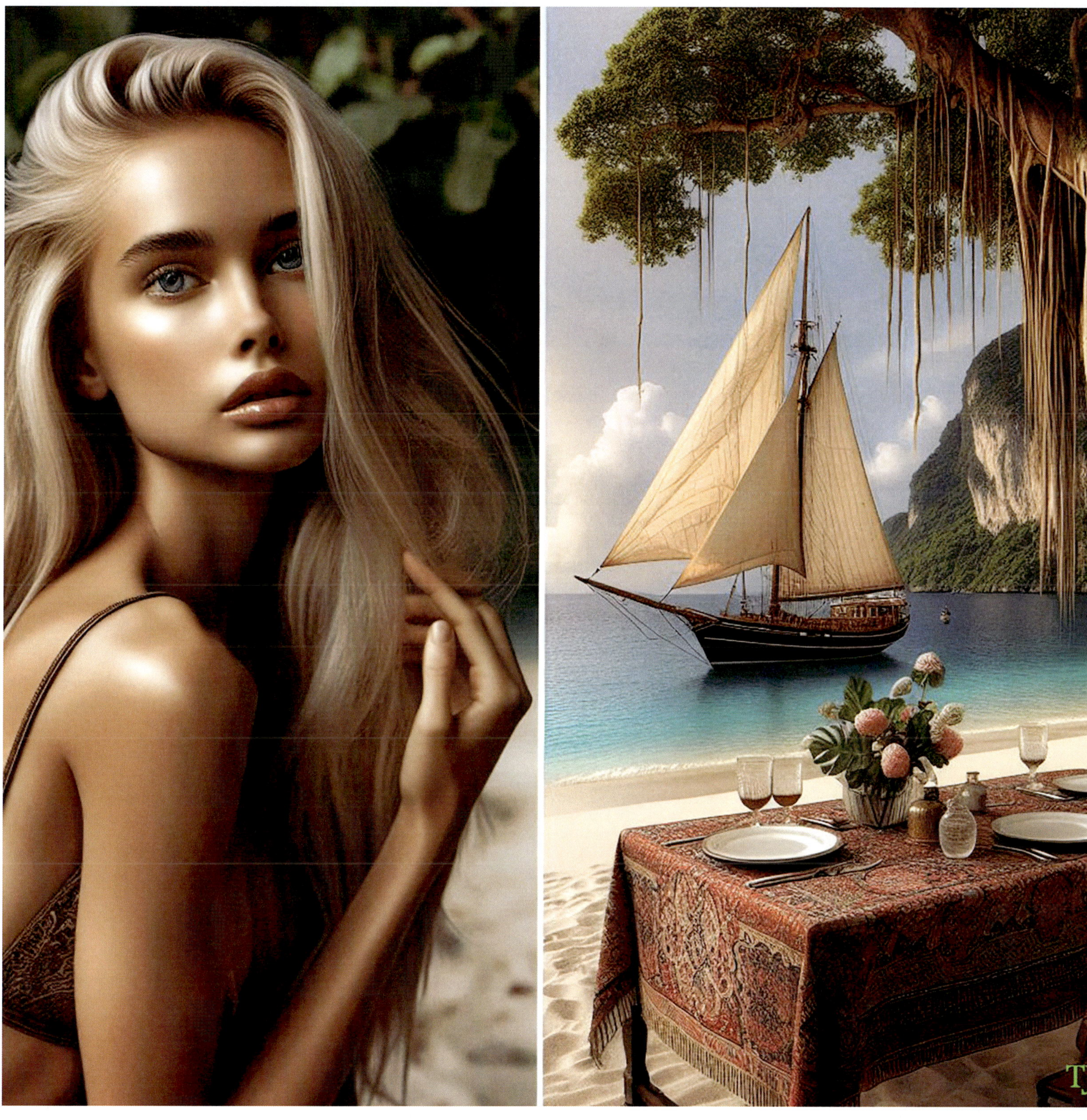

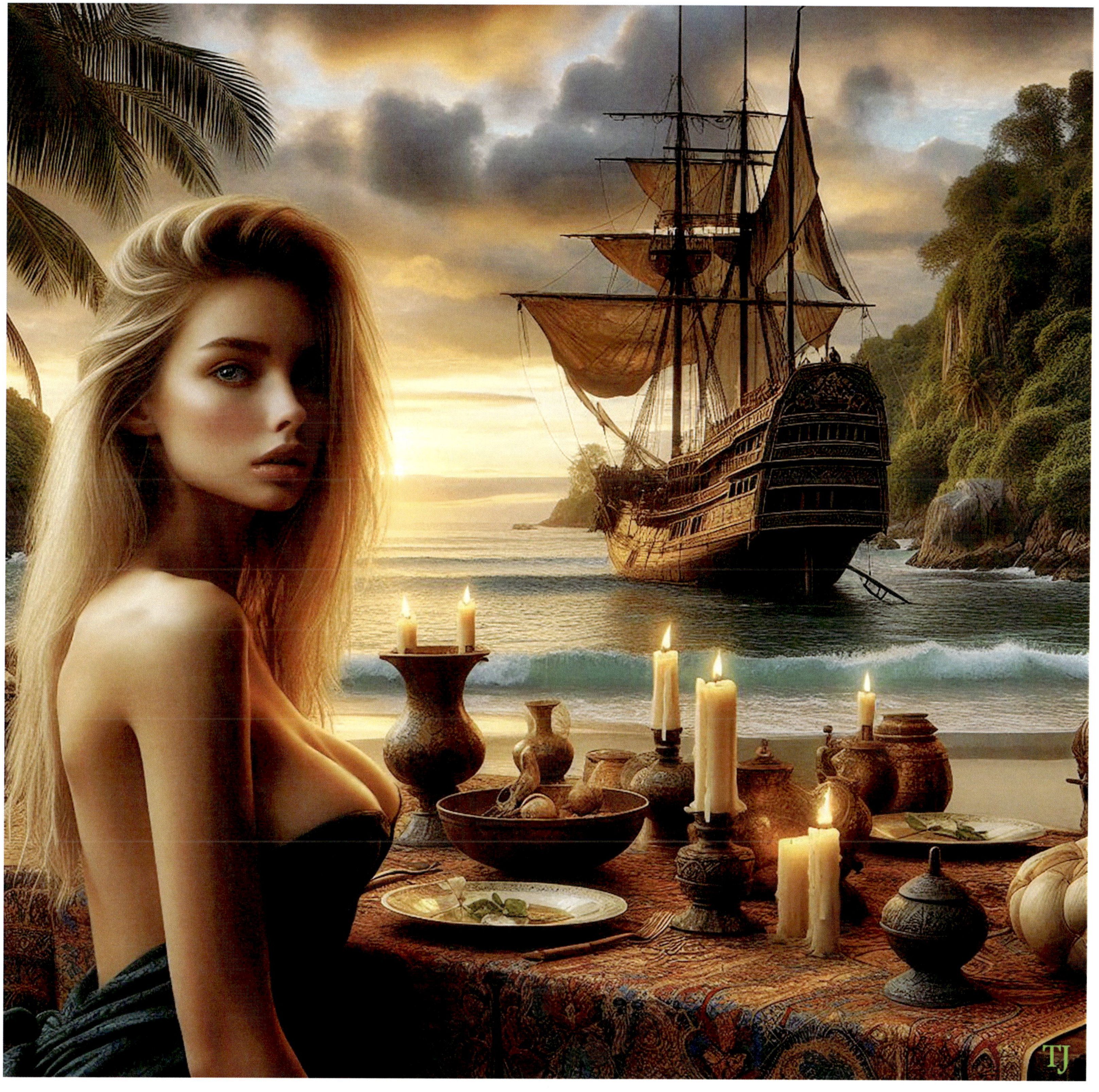

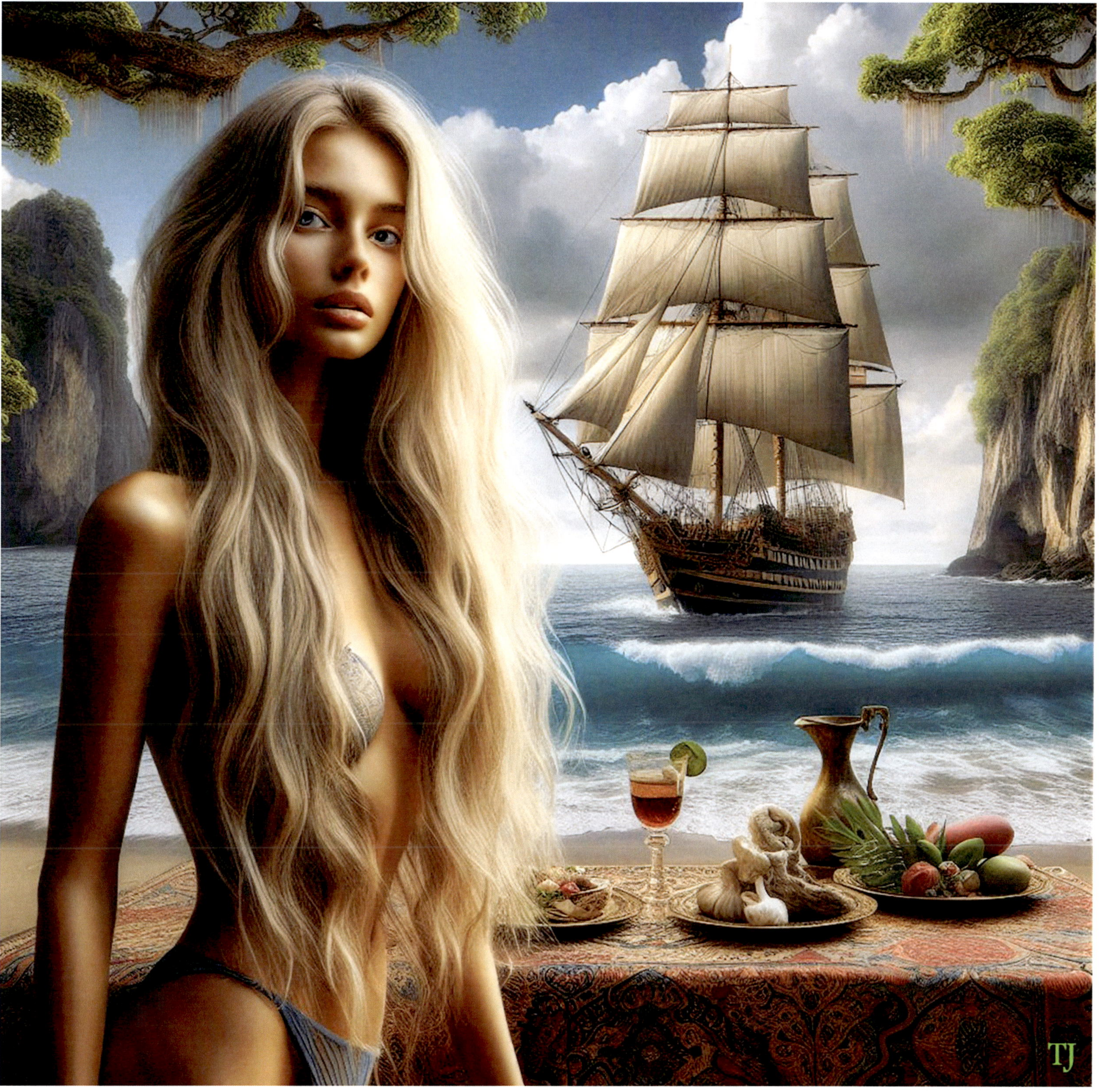
TJ

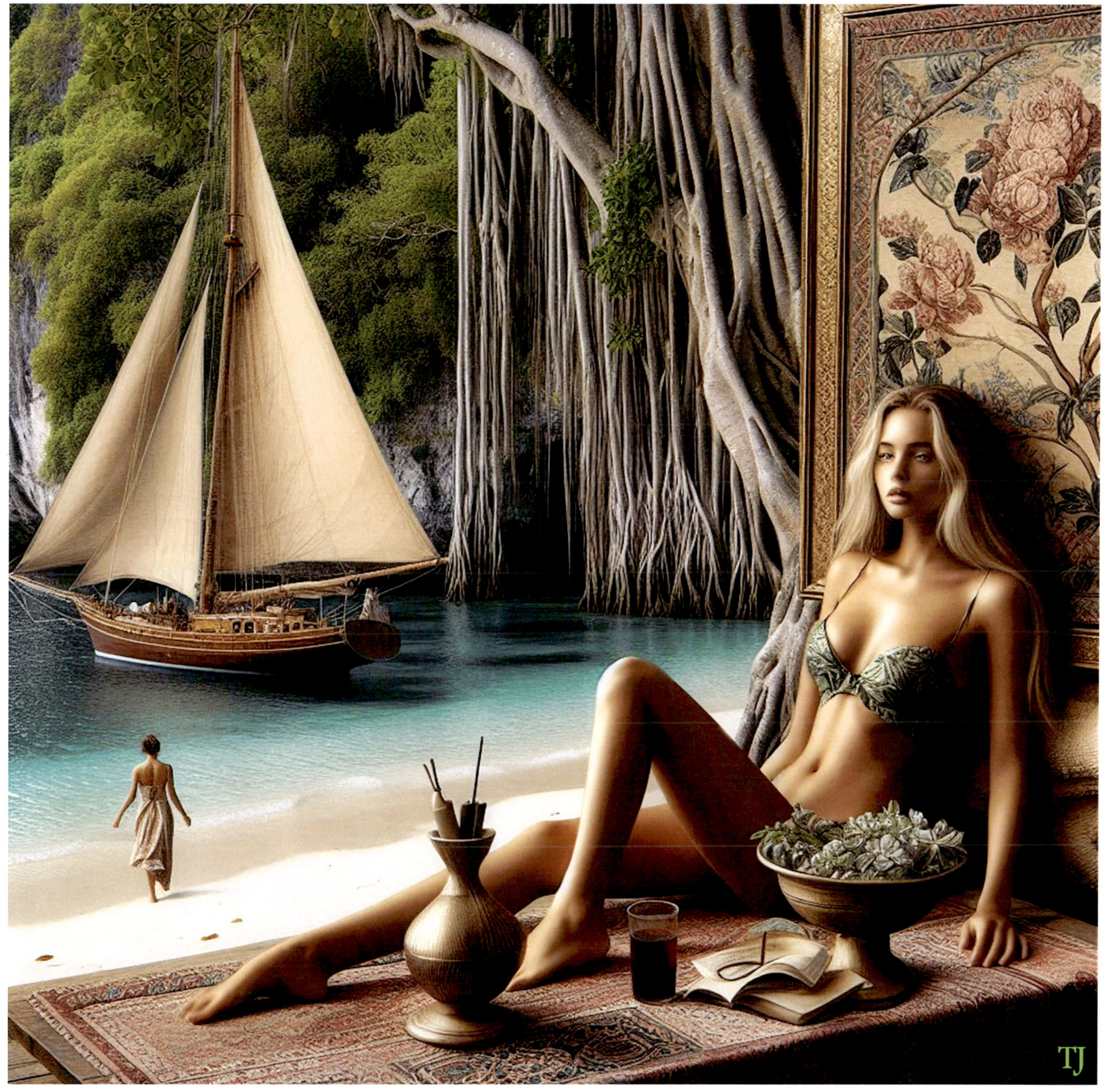

TJ

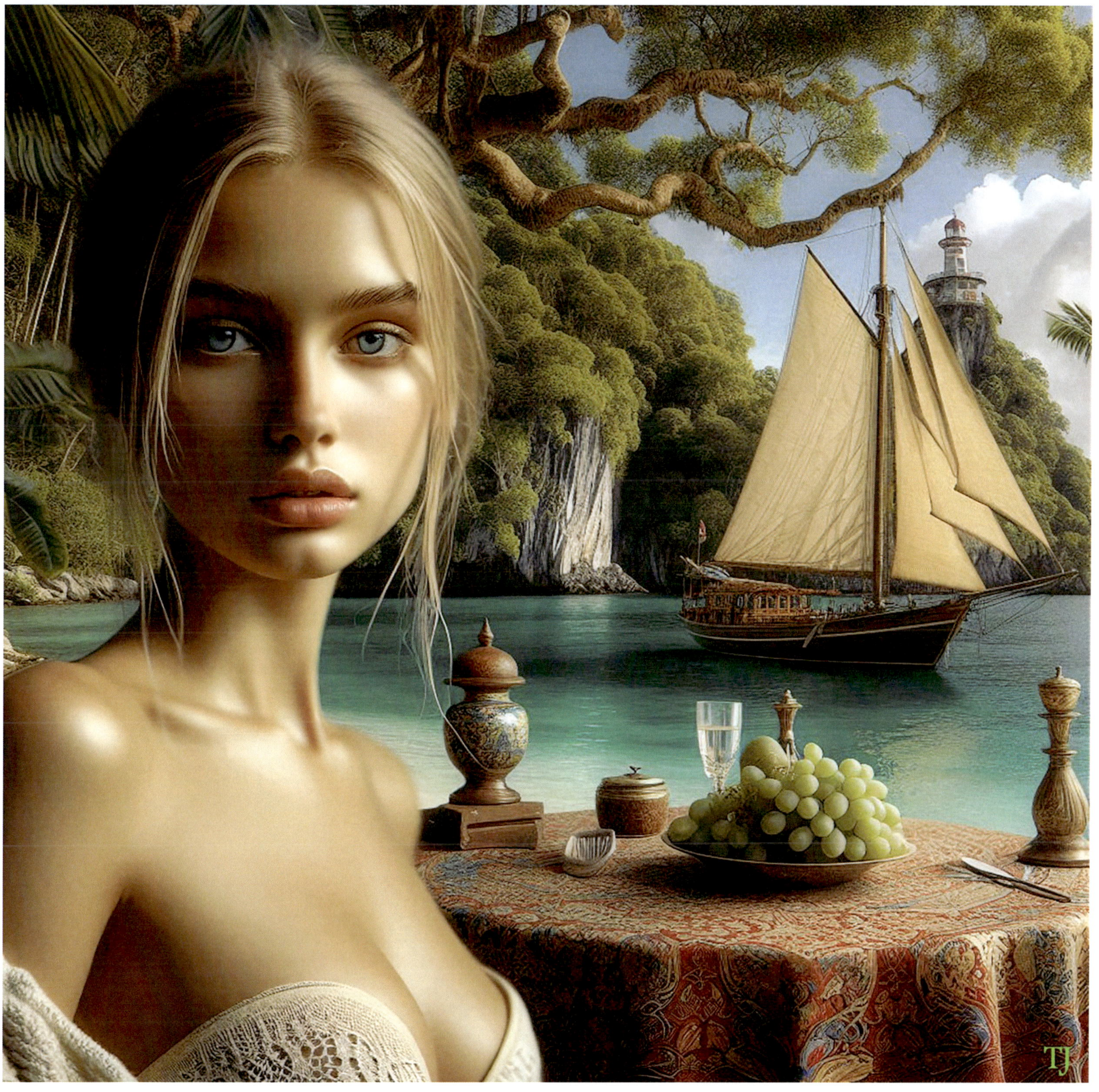
TJ

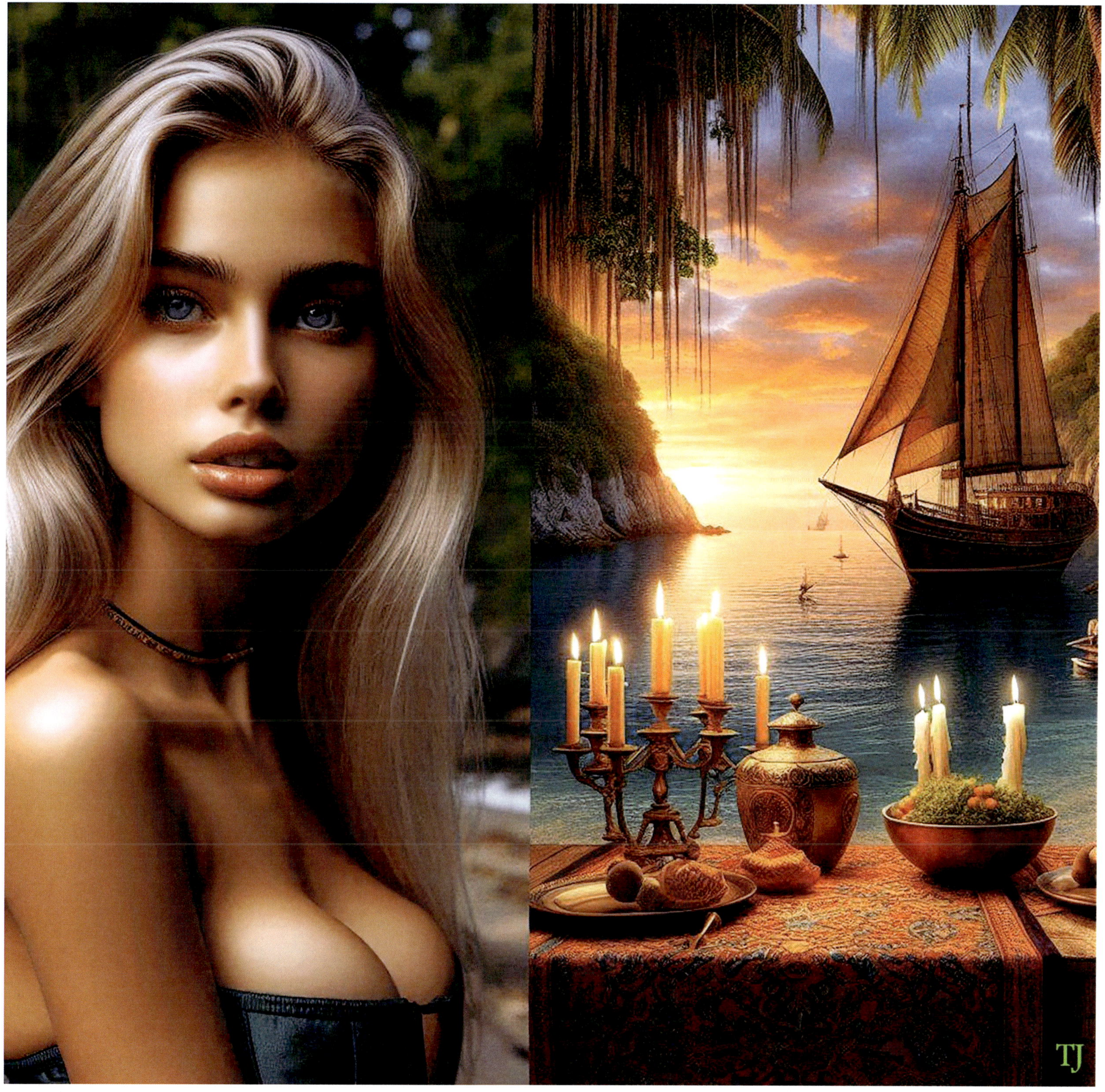

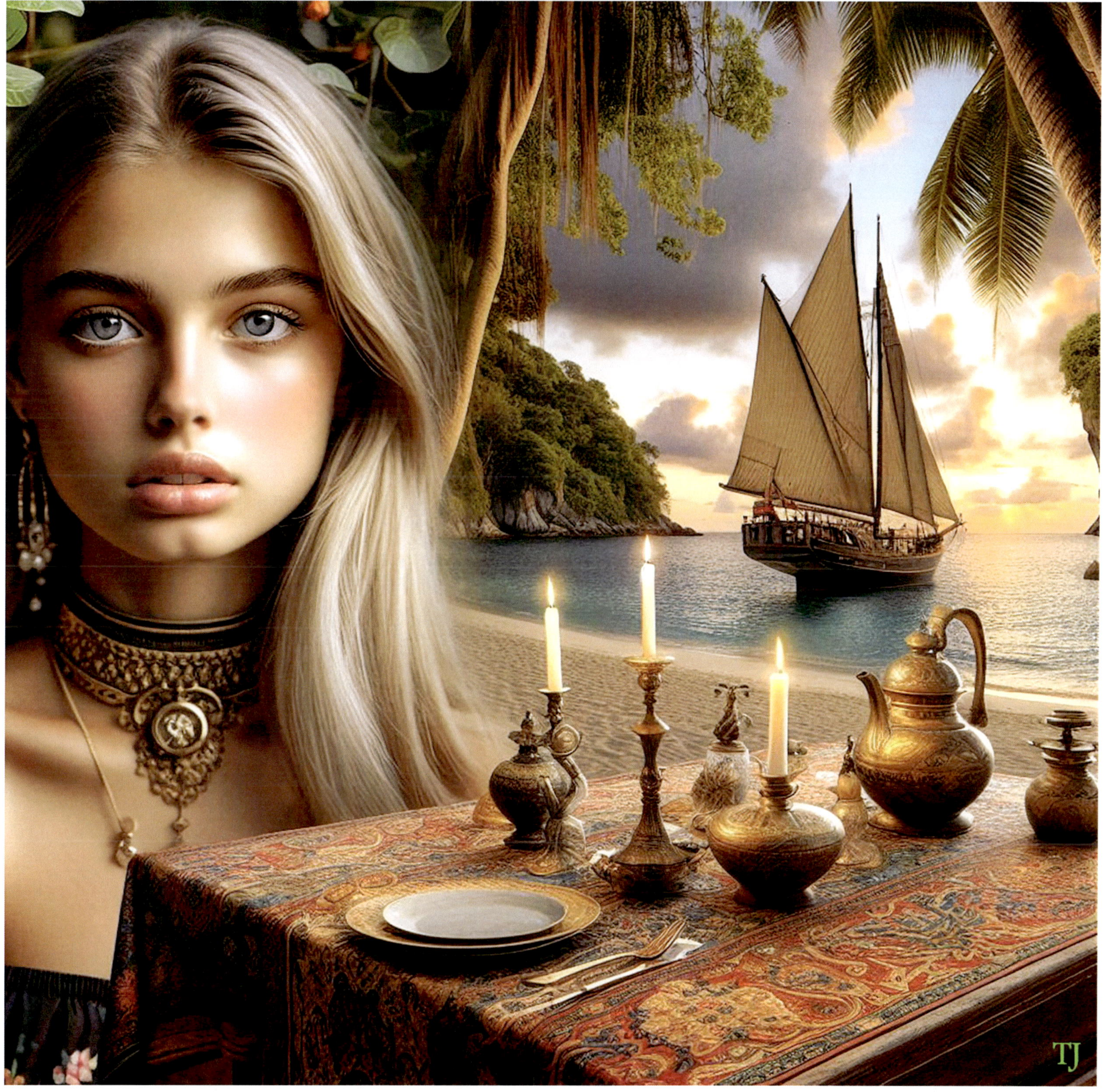

TJ

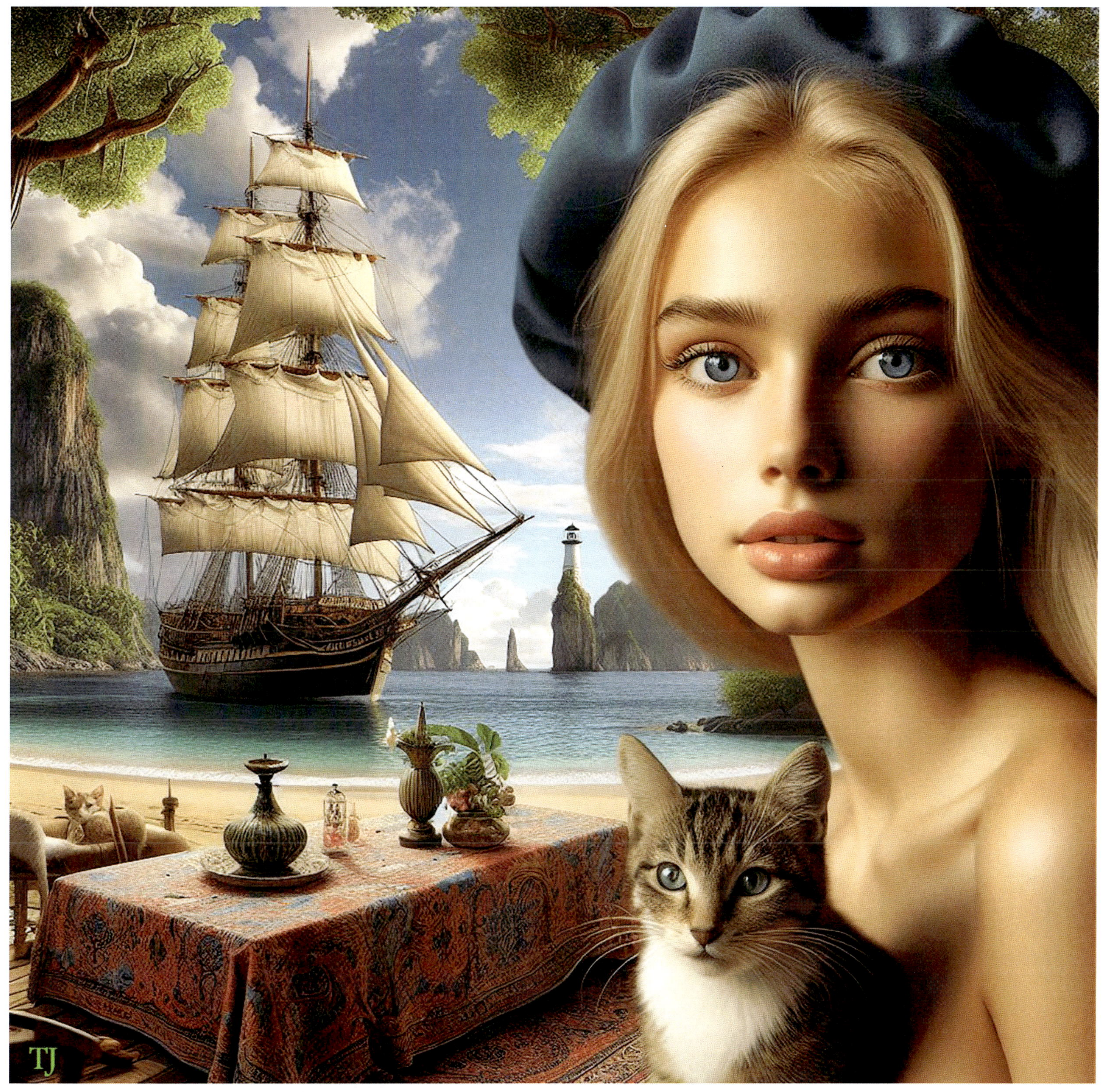
TJ

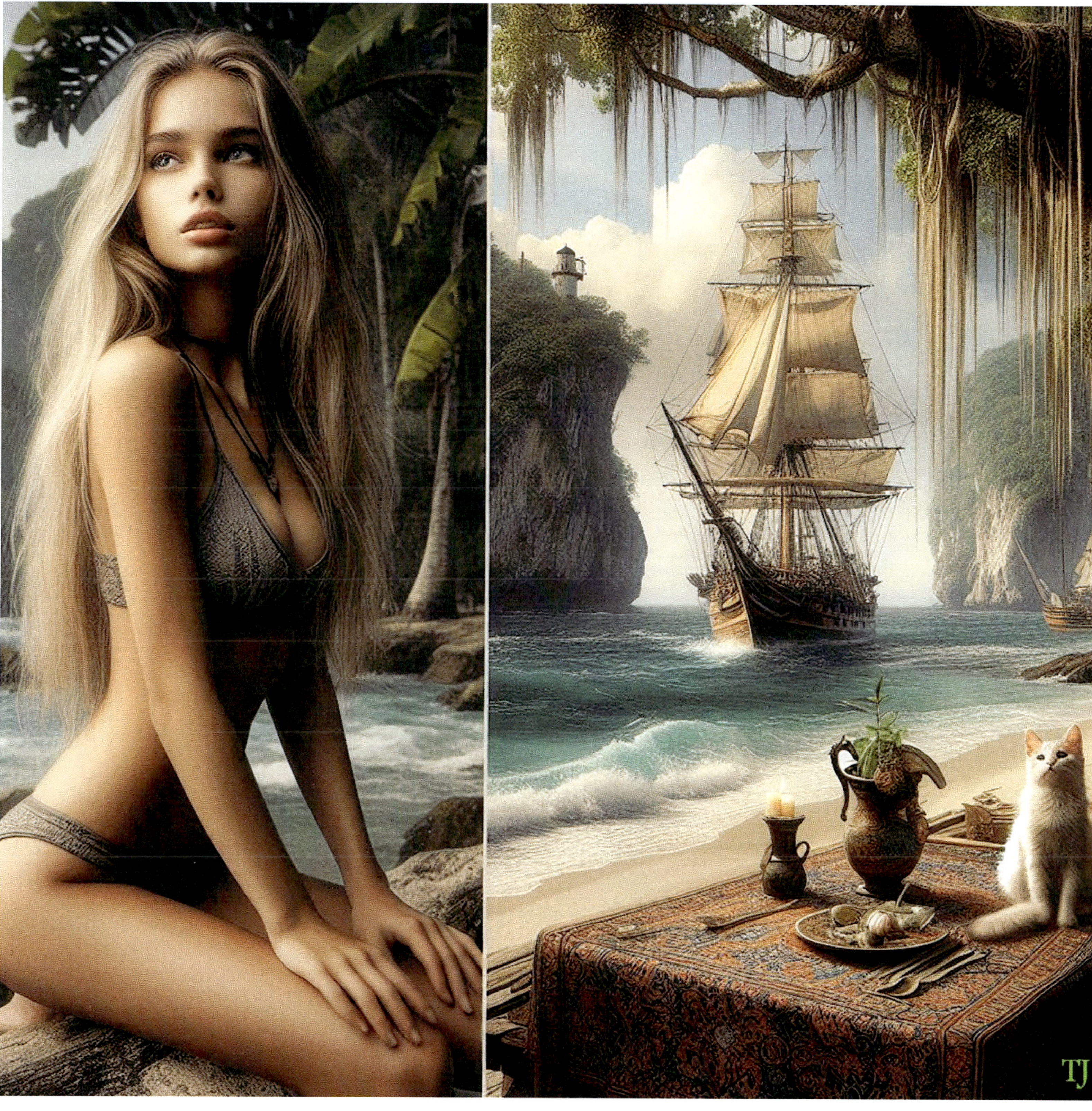

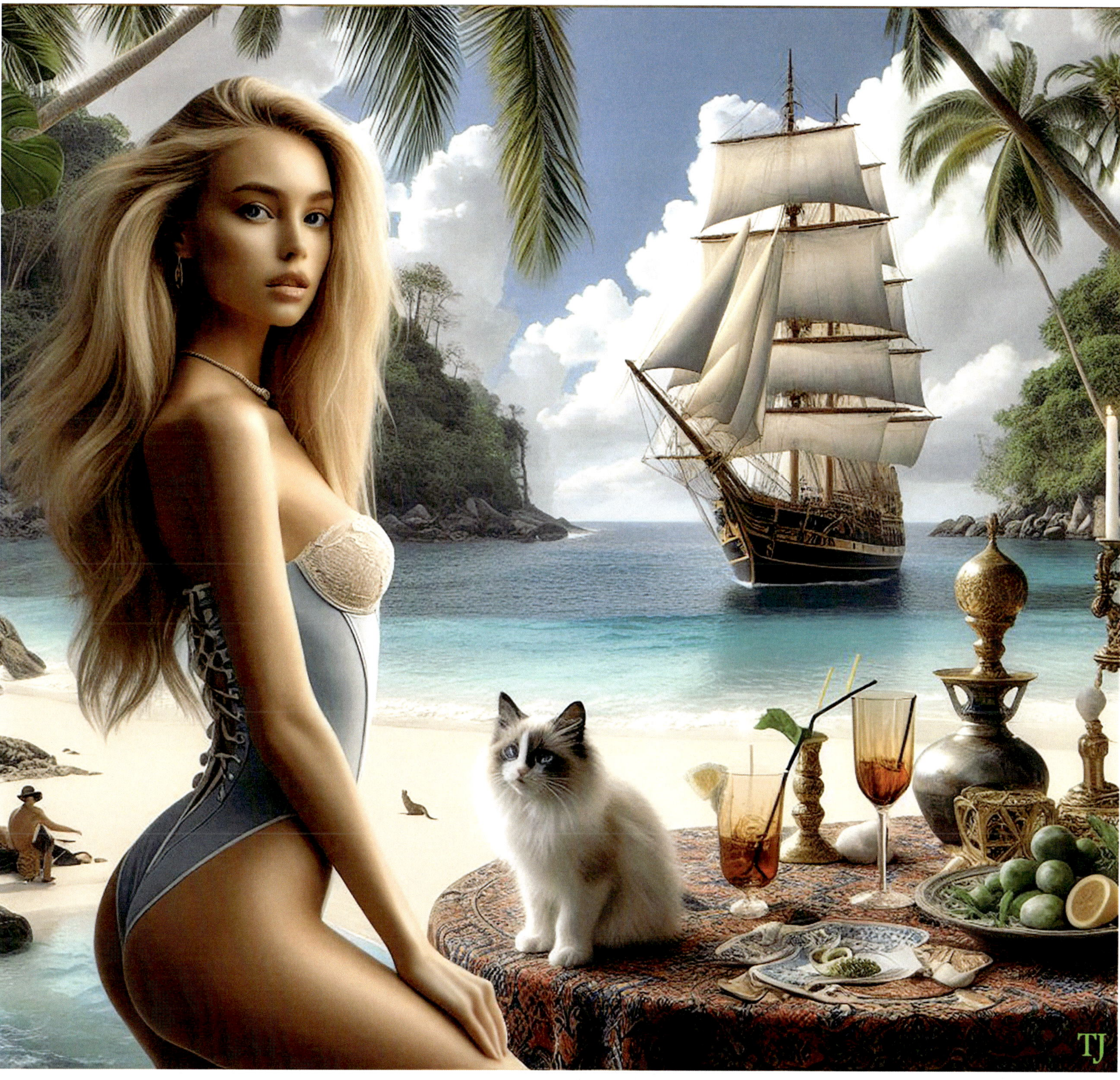
TJ

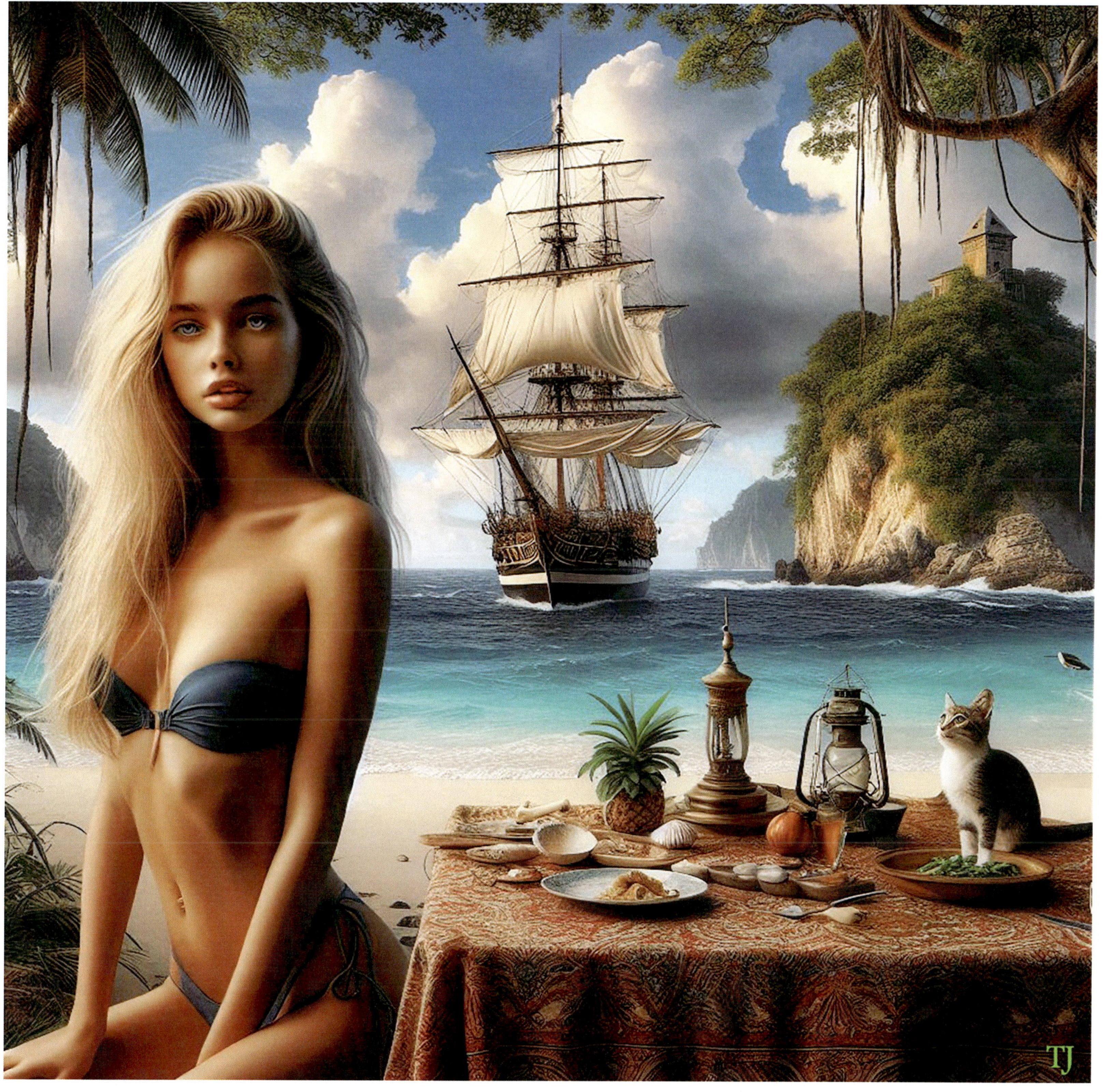

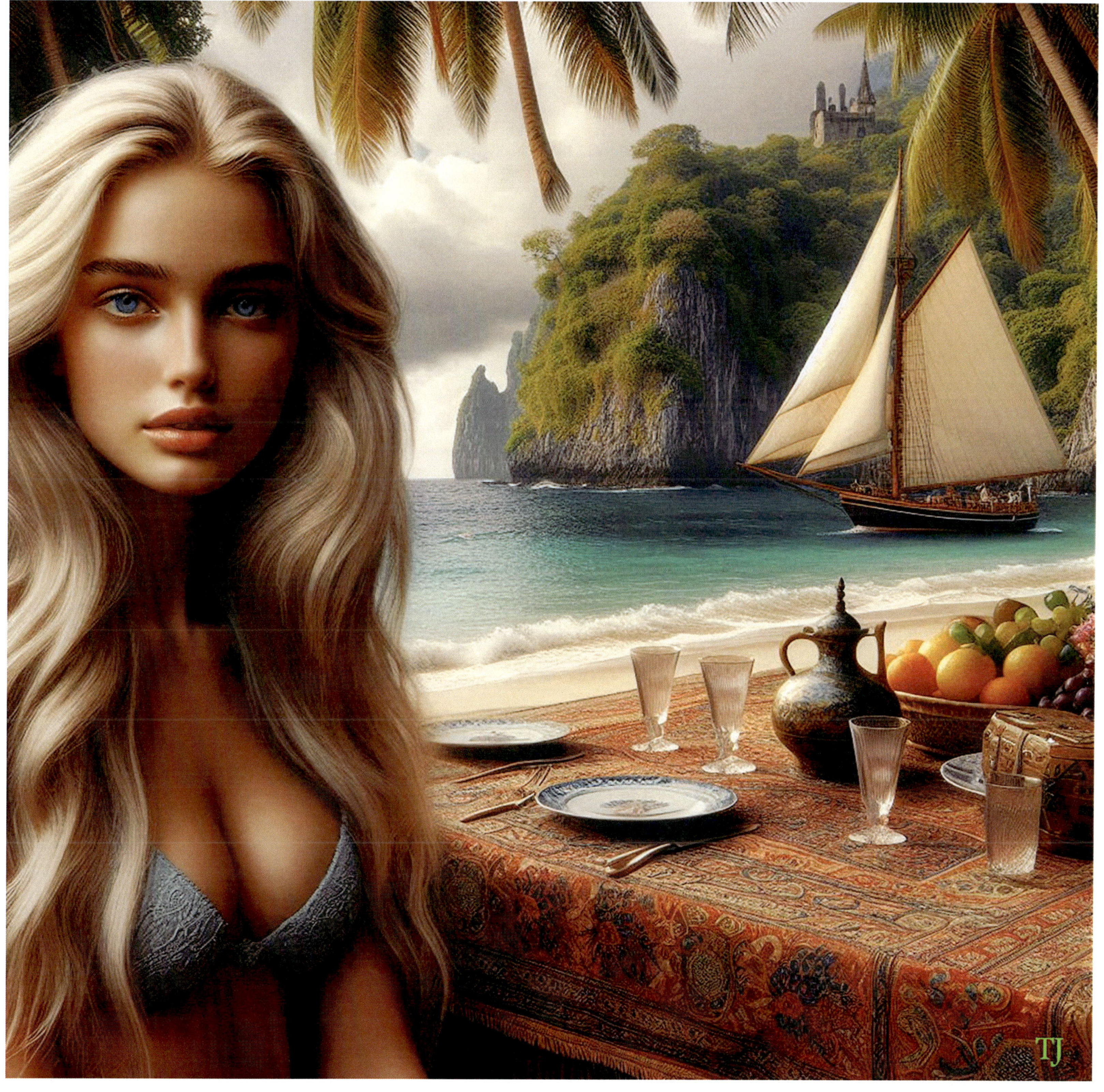
TJ

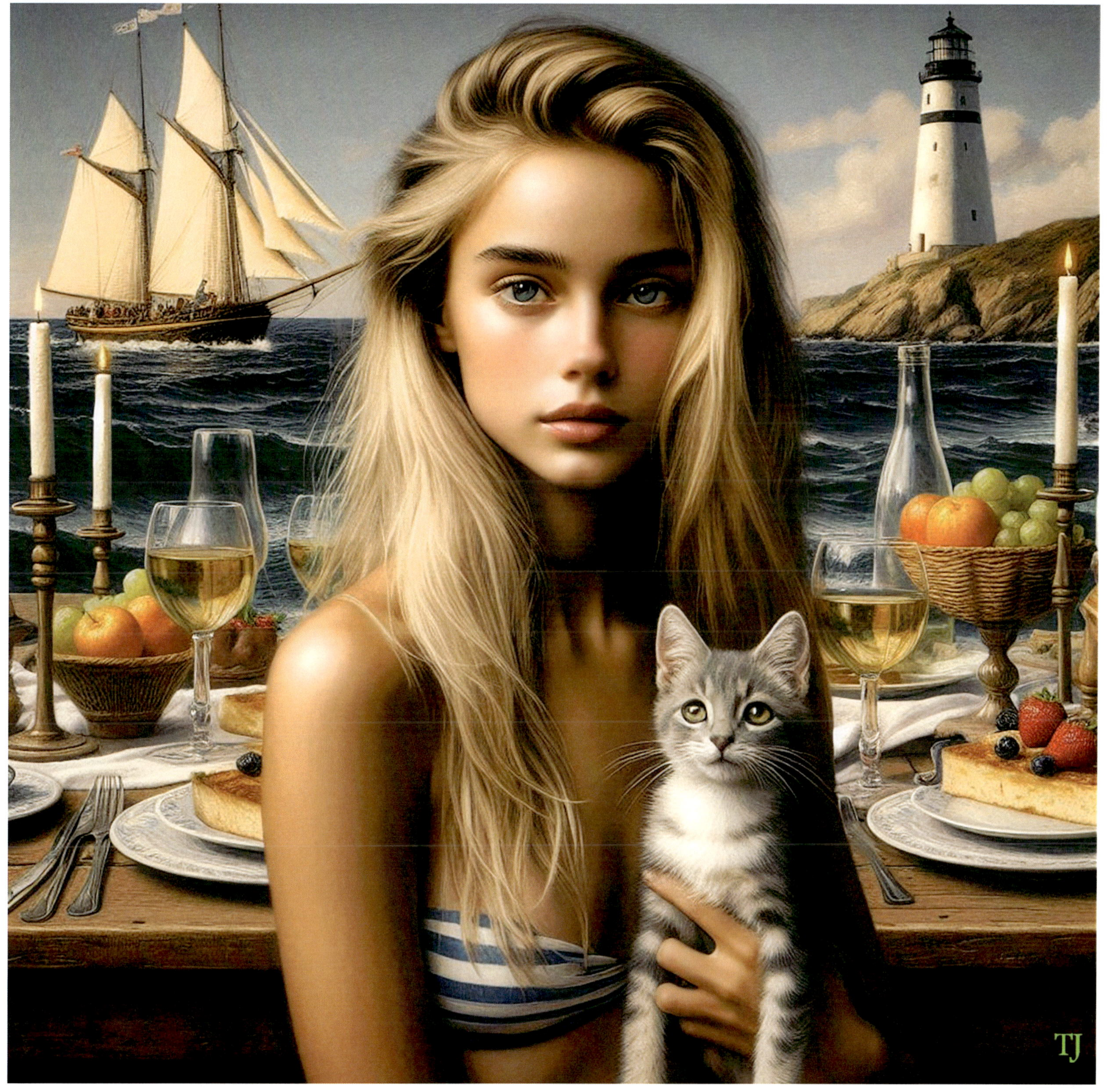
TJ

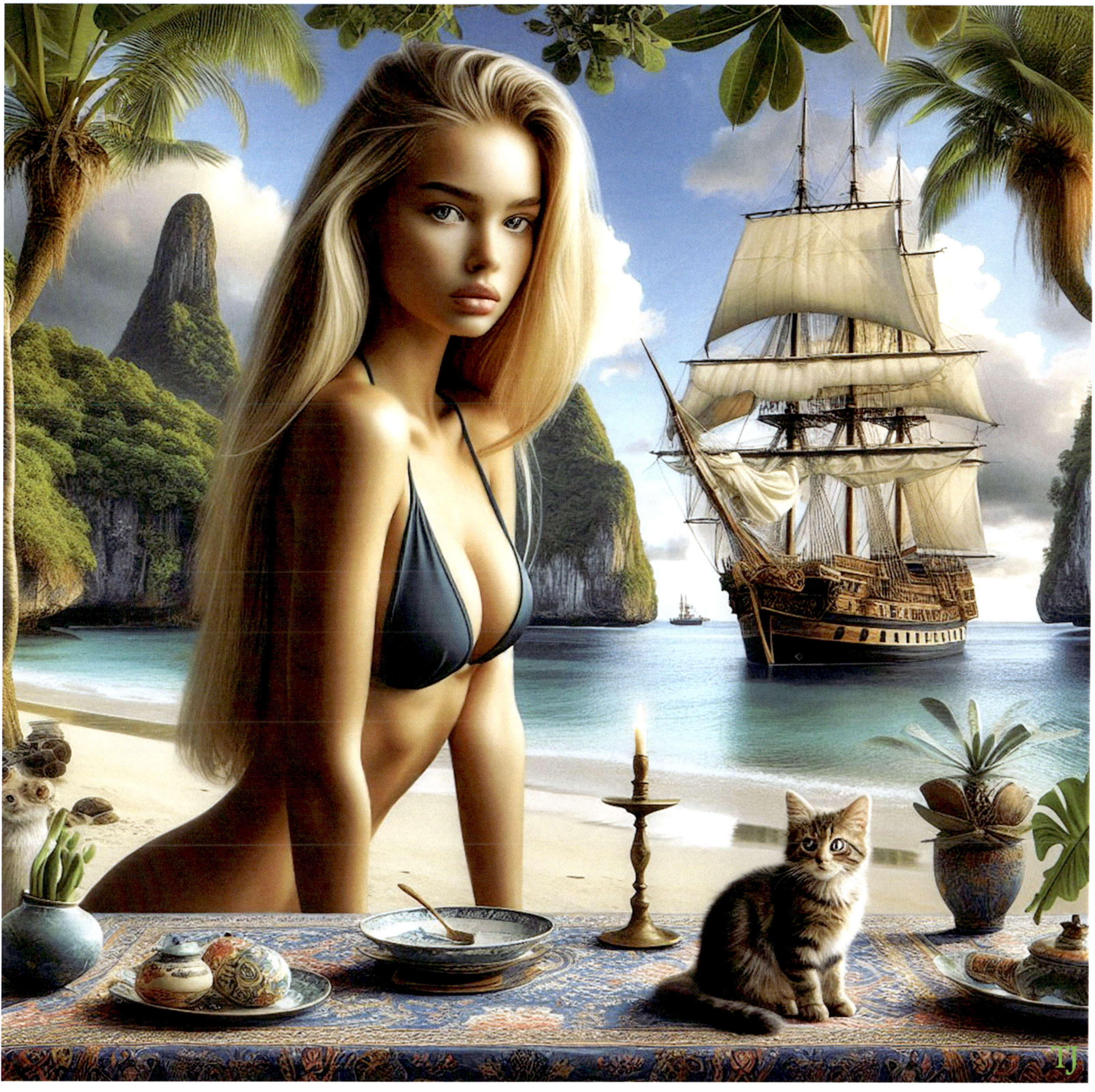

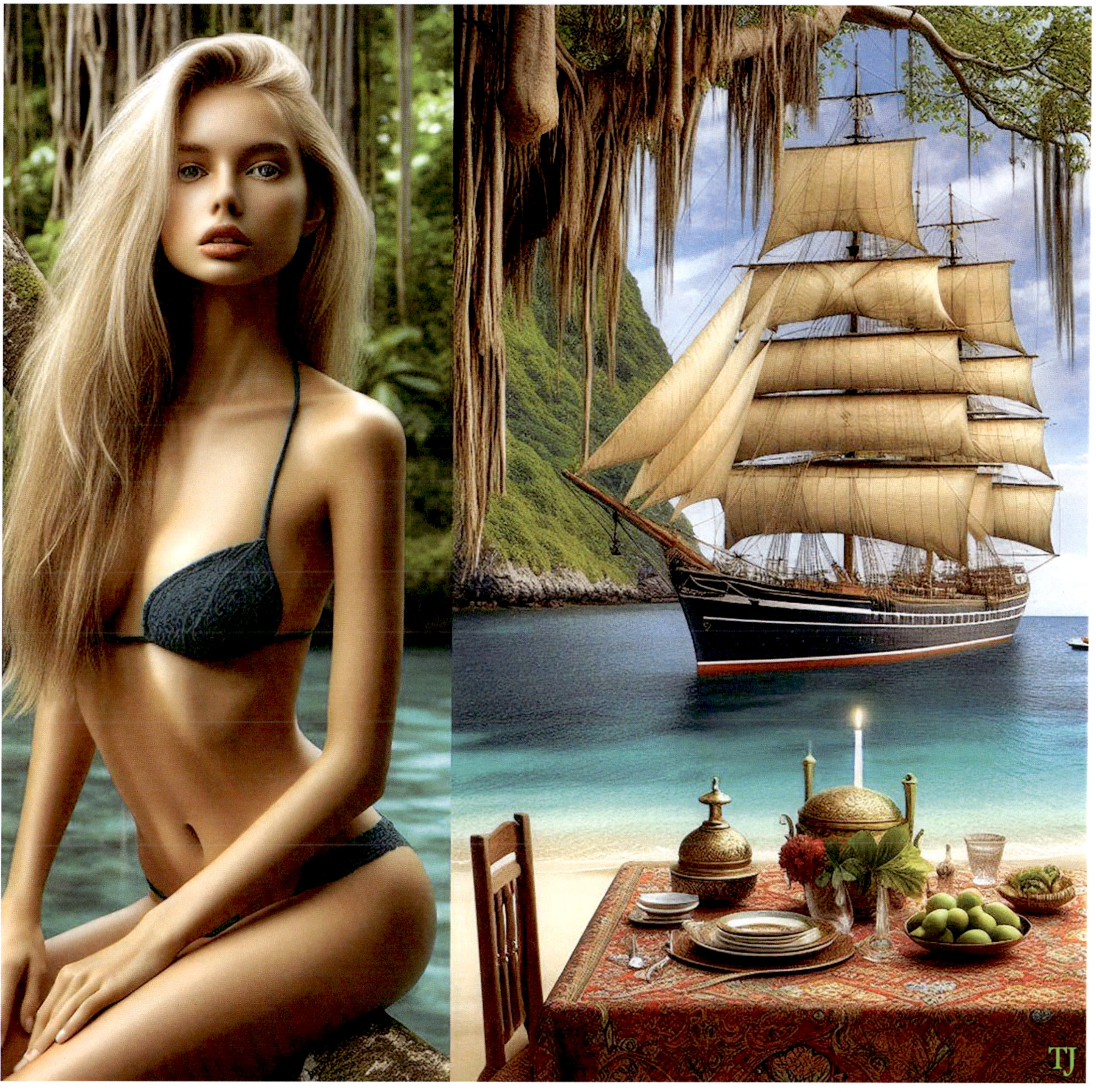

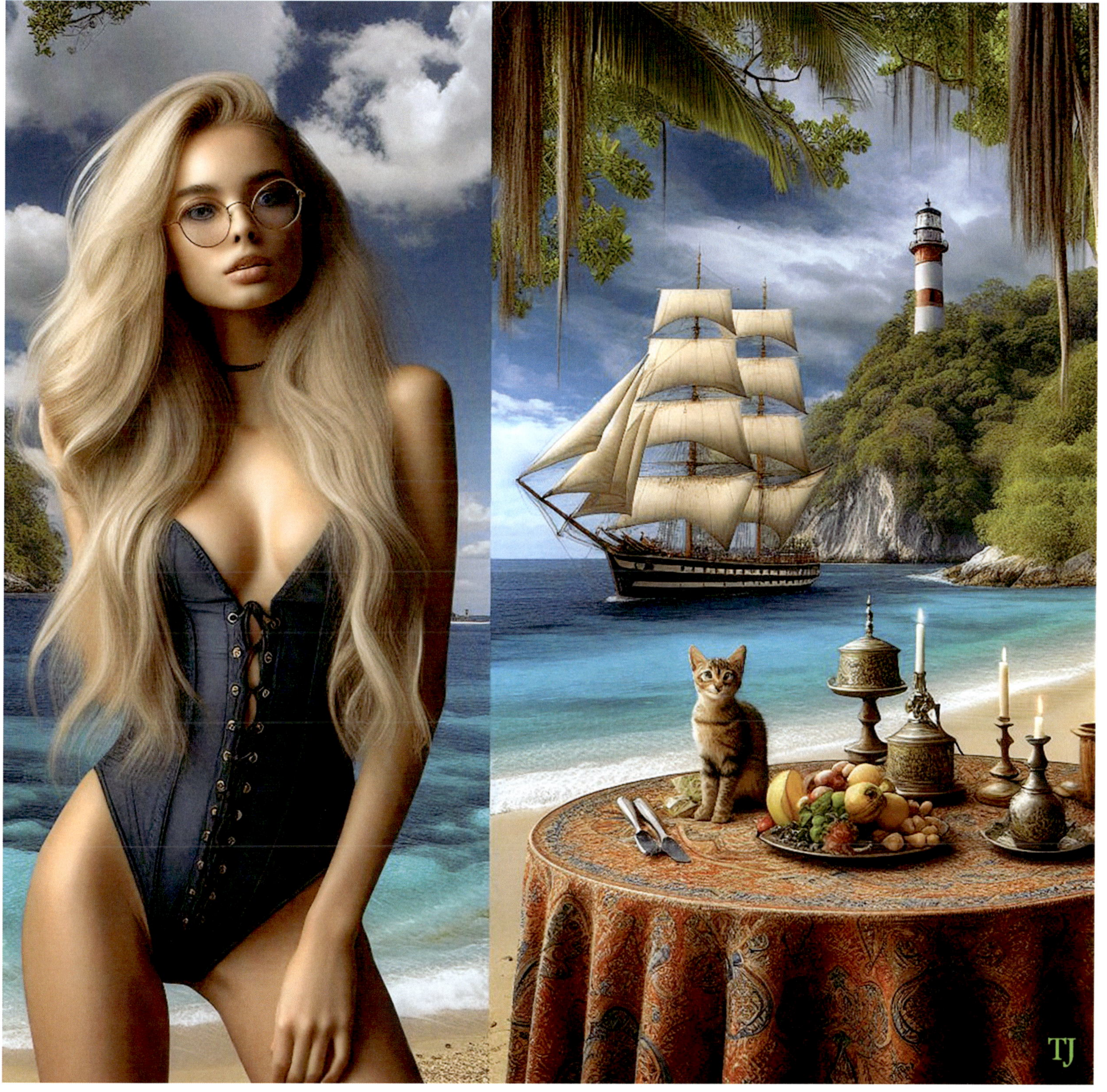

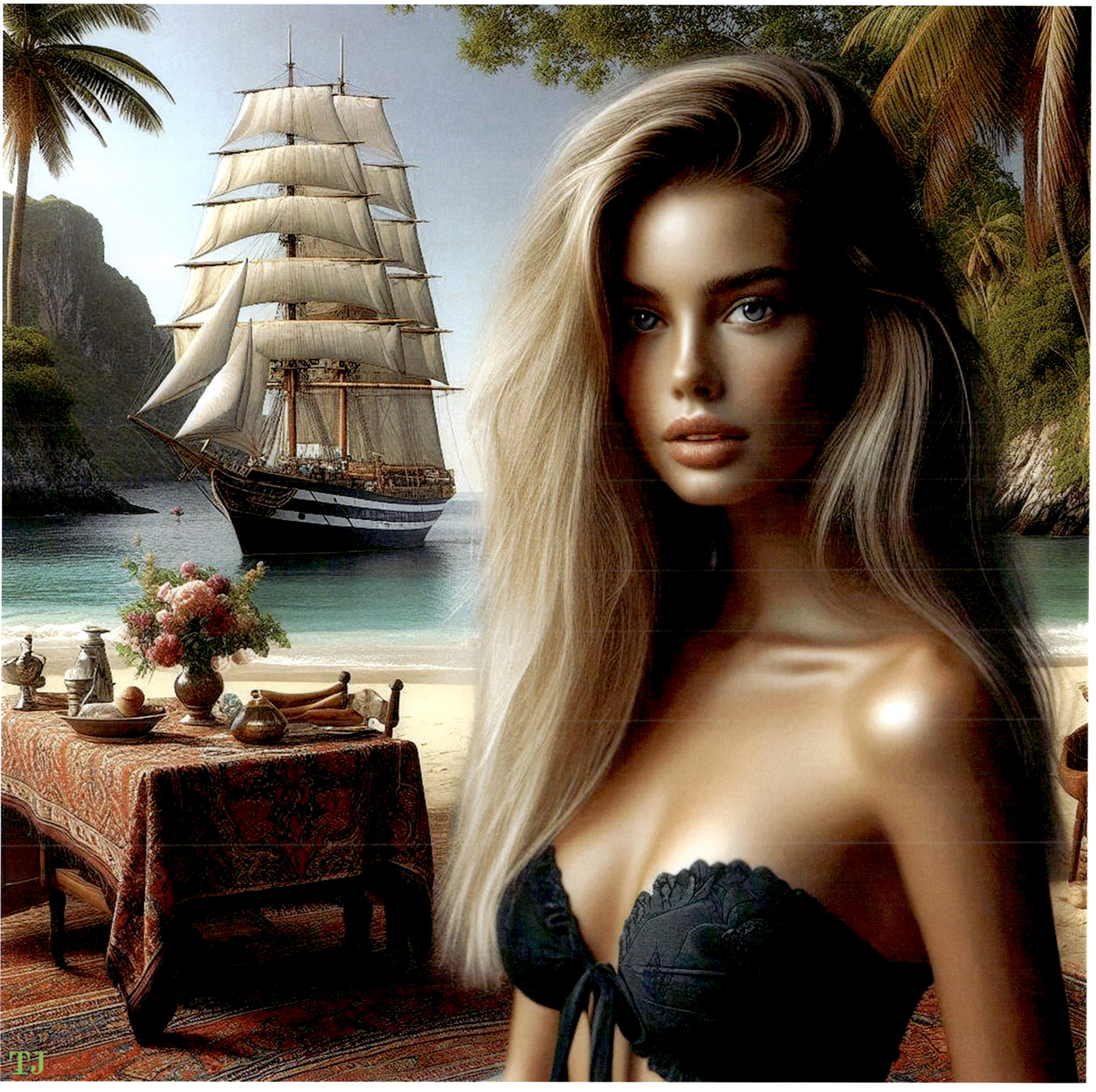
TJ

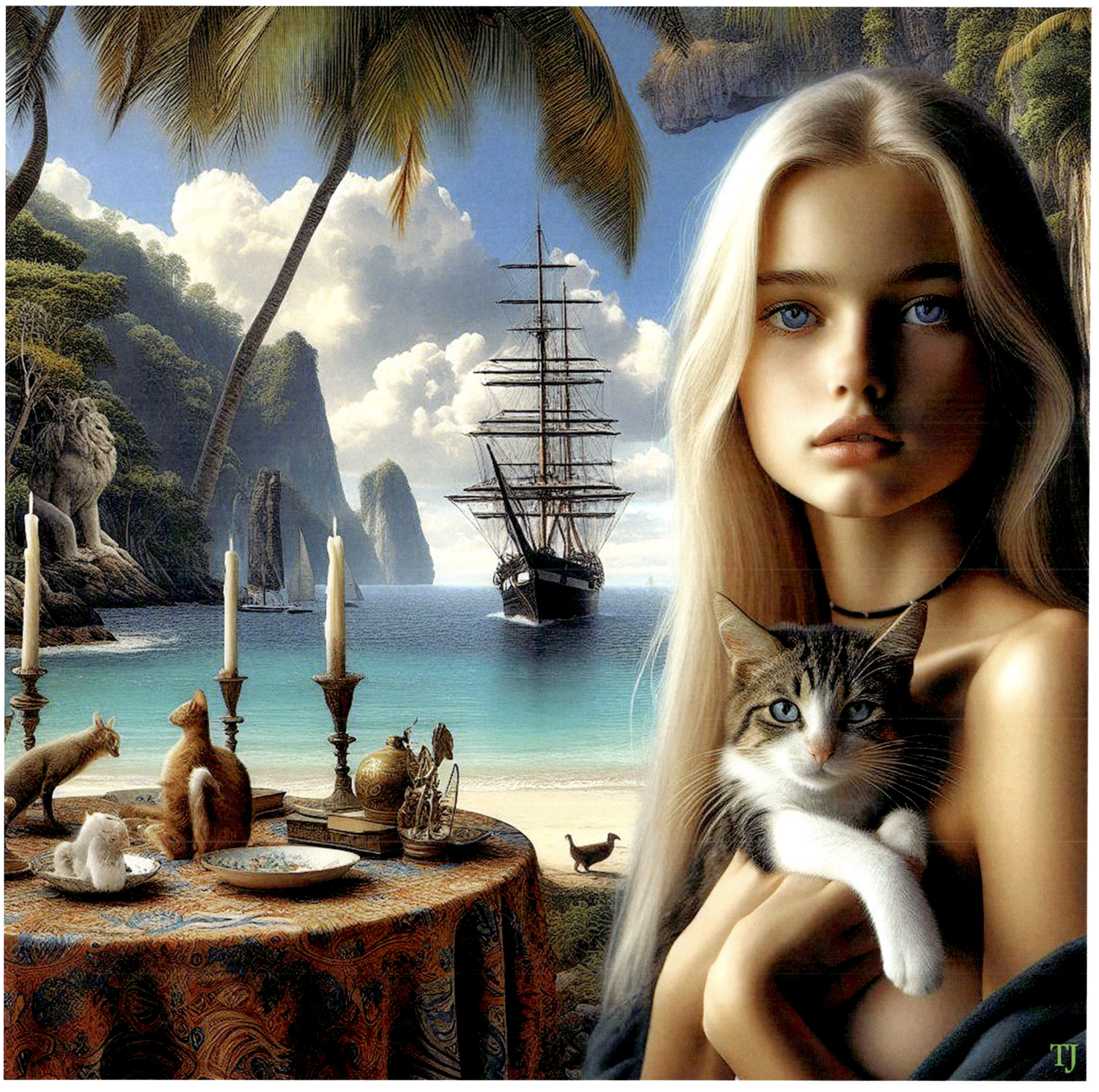

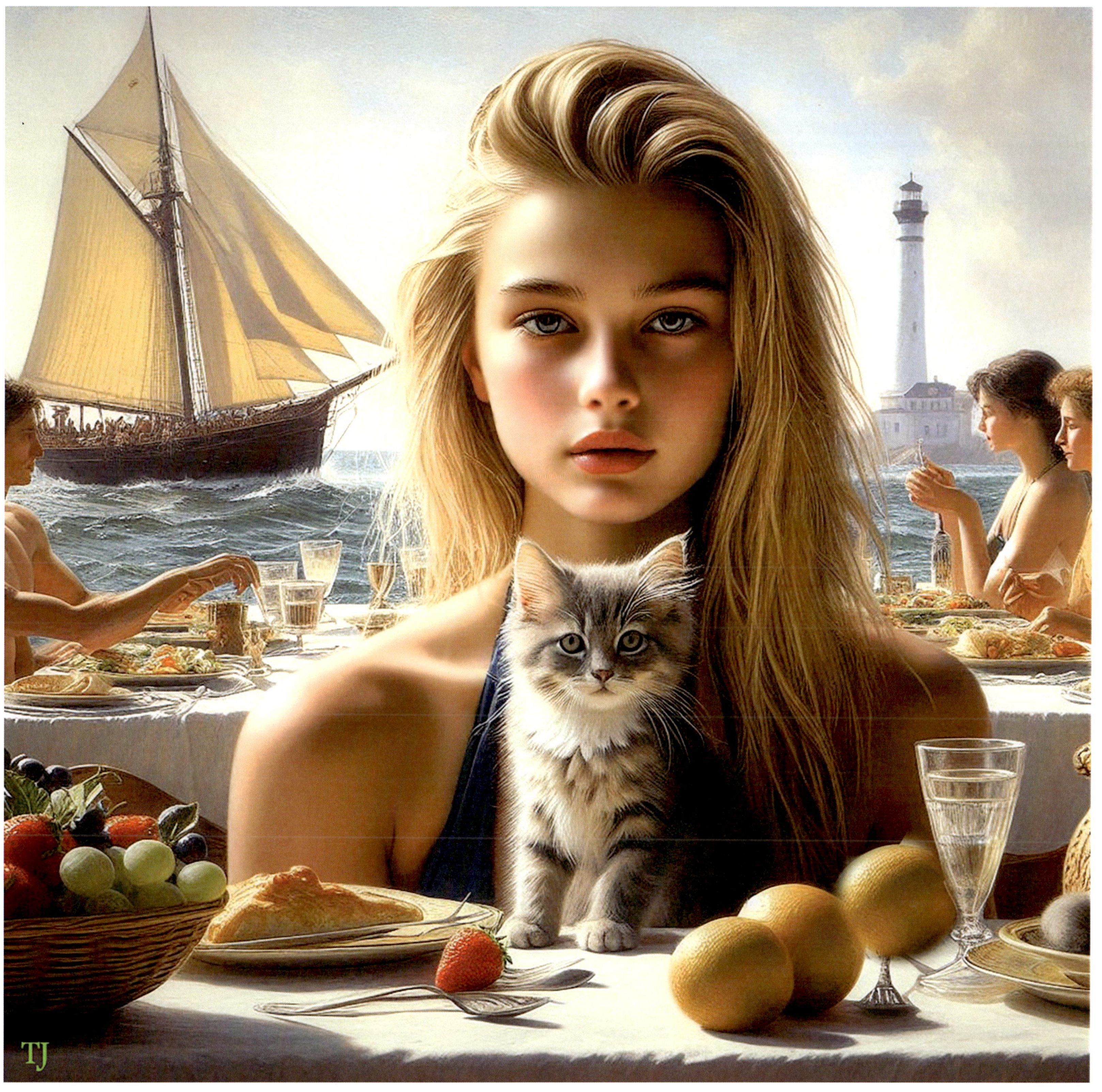
TJ

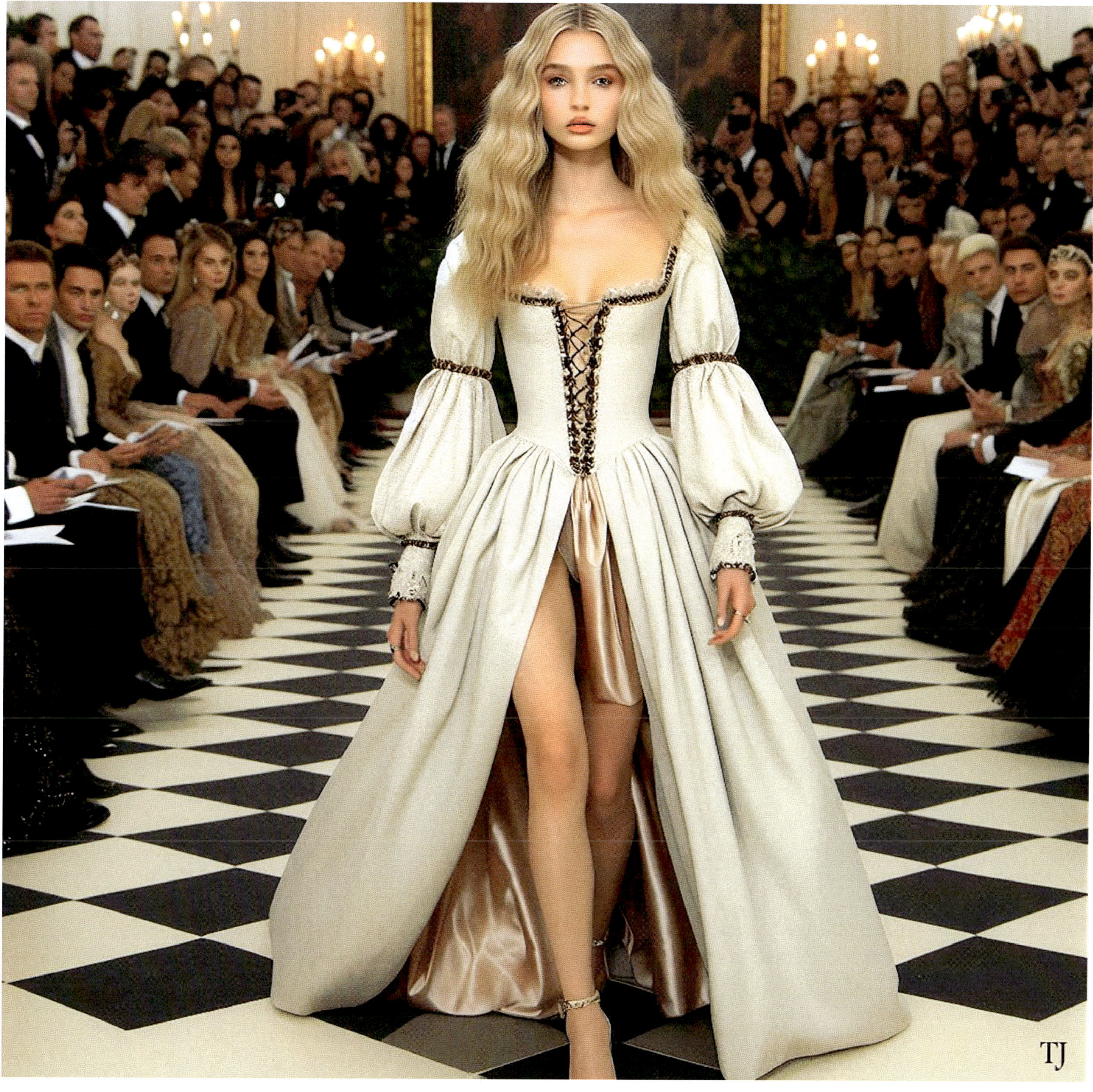

TJ

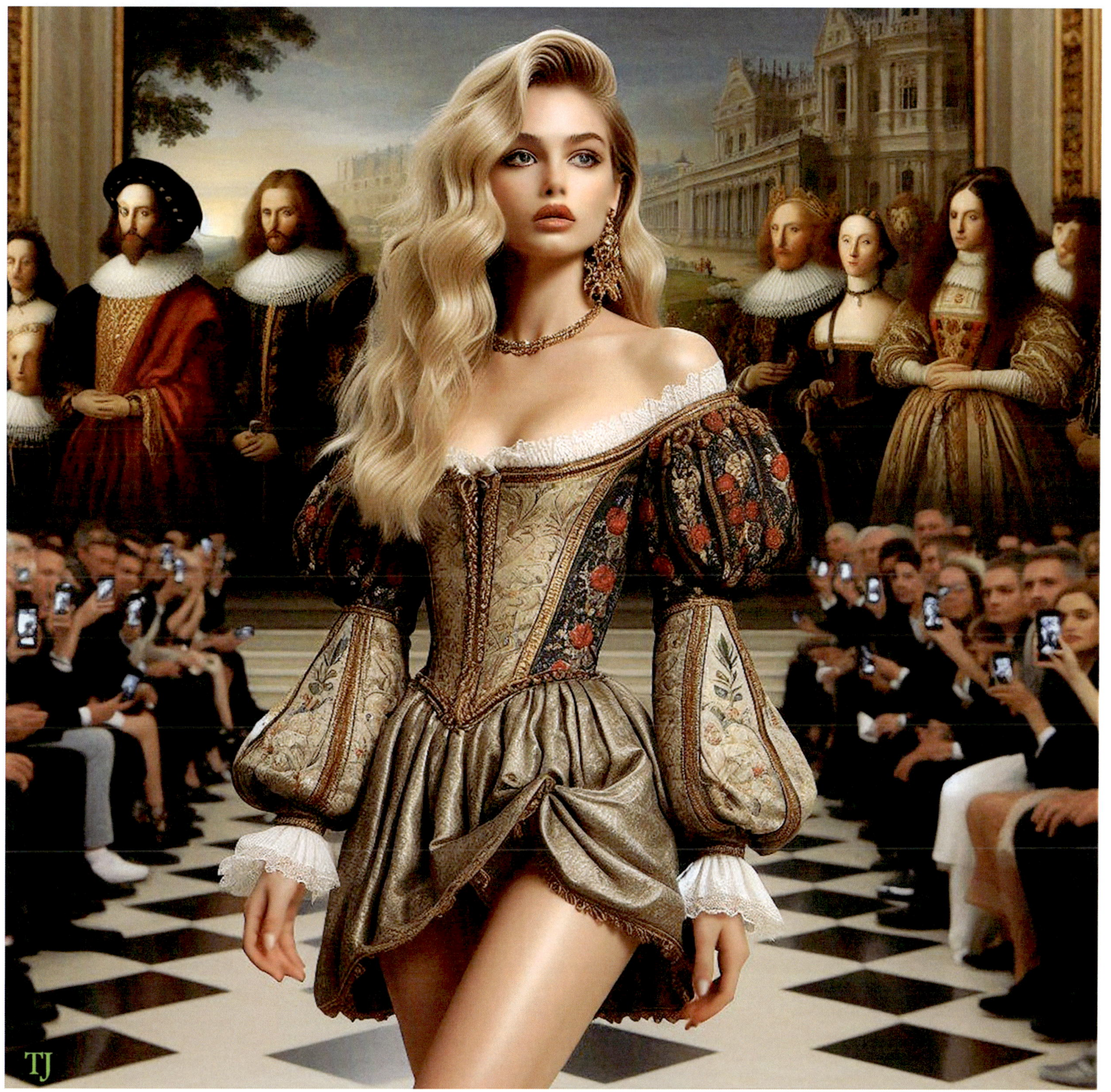
TJ

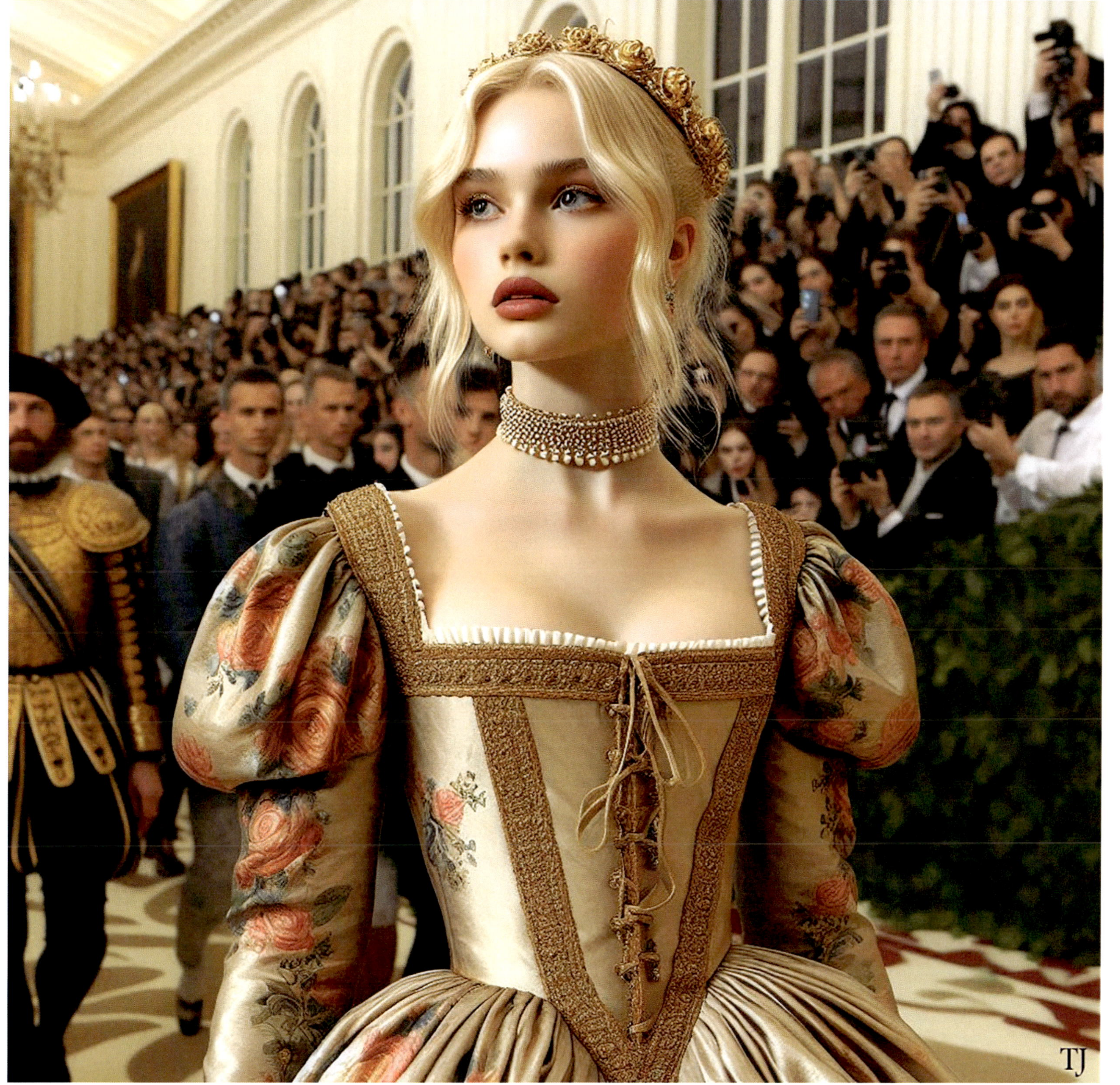
TJ

9 798999 128515 5